Is Whistleblowing a Duty?

Political Theory Today

Emanuela Ceva
Michele Bocchiola

Is Whistleblowing a Duty?

polity

First published in 2019 by Polity Press

Polity Press
65 Bridge Street
Cambridge CB2 1UR, UK

Polity Press
101 Station Landing
Suite 300
Medford, MA 02155, USA

ISBN-13: 978-1-5095-2965-0
ISBN-13: 978-1-5095-2966-7 (pb)

A catalogue record for this book is available from the British Library.

Library of Congress Cataloging-in-Publication Data

Names: Ceva, Emanuela, author. | Bocchiola, Michele, author.
Title: Is whistleblowing a duty? / Emanuela Ceva, Michele Bocchiola.
Other titles: Is whistle blowing a duty?
Description: Cambridge, UK ; Medford, MA, USA : Polity Press, 2018. |
   Includes bibliographical references and index.
Identifiers: LCCN 2018022731 (print) | LCCN 2018038958 (ebook) | ISBN
   9781509529681 (Epub) | ISBN 9781509529650 | ISBN 9781509529667 (pb)
Subjects: LCSH: Whistle blowing--Moral and ethical aspects.
Classification: LCC JF1525.W45 (ebook) | LCC JF1525.W45 C39 2018 (print) |
   DDC 174/.4--dc23
LC record available at https://lccn.loc.gov/2018022731

Typeset in 11 on 15 Sabon by Servis Filmsetting Ltd, Stockport, Cheshire
Printed and bound in the United Kingdom by Clays Ltd, Elcograf S.p.A.

For further information on Polity, visit our website: politybooks.com

Contents

Acknowledgements

Chapters of this book were presented at the Association for Social and Political Philosophy Annual Conference at the University of Sheffield (2017) and the International Colloquium on 'The Democratic Legitimacy of State Secrecy' at the University of Leiden (2017). We would like to thank the participants for their helpful feedback. The entire manuscript was the object of a dedicated workshop at Northeastern University in January 2018; we are very grateful to Candice Delmas for organizing this event and for her active engagement in it.

We would also like to thank the three anonymous referees, along with the Editors of Polity Press, for their valuable remarks and encouraging suggestions at several stages of the writing process. For their comments on previous versions of some of the chapters,

Acknowledgements

we owe a debt of gratitude to Eric Boot, Francesco Chiesa, Chiara Cordelli, Candice Delmas, Mark Fenster, Maria Paola Ferretti, Manohar Kumar, Dorota Mokrosińska, Gianfranco Pellegrino, Rahul Sagar, Daniele Santoro, William Smith, Bruno Verbeek, Wim Vandekerckhove, Mark Warren, and Federico Zuolo.

A large part of the manuscript was written while Emanuela Ceva was a Fulbright Scholar at the Edmund J. Safra Center for Ethics at Harvard University. She is grateful to the Fulbright Commission for the opportunity, and to the Center for providing the most congenial and supportive environment for developing the arguments in the book.

The research for this paper was carried out with the financial support of the European Commission Internal Security Fund Project 'A Change of Direction', GA: HOME/2014/ISFP/AG/EFCE/7233.

The book is dedicated to our partners, Andrea and Ania, for their unfaltering support and for graciously accepting their shared fate as impromptu test-beds for our thought experiments.

Introduction

Imagine someone within the organization for which you work is engaged in a potentially illicit activity. Say she uses the company's car to drive her husband to work every day. What would you do if you found out? Would you say nothing? Would you share your concerns with somebody? Would you confront your colleague directly, or would you turn to someone else within the organization, perhaps your supervisor?

Surely, your decision depends significantly on the activity in question. Let us say that, to be relevant, your colleague's activity must involve some kind of wrongdoing. Unfortunately, 'wrongdoing' is a vague term that includes both crimes and misdemeanours (i.e., wrongful behaviours prohibited by the law) and ethically problematic but not necessarily illegal behaviours (i.e., actions contrary to

1

moral norms or principles of justice). But we could also add to the list apparently trivial actions such as petty violations of norms of etiquette.

This uncertainty aside, suppose that, after careful consideration, you decide you should report your colleague's behaviour because, although not unlawful, it is unfair to the company; so you go and talk to your supervisor about it. What if she does not listen to you? Would you then talk to other colleagues? Would you report what you know to the police or leak information to the media? On the one hand, if you decide to do so, you must be aware of the risk of upsetting your supervisor – who could then retaliate against your 'disloyalty' – and your other colleagues, who might isolate you and treat you as a spy. You should also consider the impact your report may have on the reputation of your organization. On the other hand, if you decide not to file any report, you know your colleague's behaviour will go unnoticed (let us assume you are the only one who has access to the company's travel log). Hence the question at the heart of this book: what should a member of an organization do when she discovers an alleged wrongdoing?

This question, or something similar to it, is what many so-called whistleblowers regularly ask themselves. Whistleblowers are members of a public or private organization who report some kind of wrongdoing, disclosing privileged information to a direct superior, to some authority, or to the public. The term 'whistleblowing' made its appearance in the public debate in the late 1950s to convey the idea of a referee who stops the action when players have committed a foul, or of a British bobby who blows his whistle to call attention to a criminal.[1] It was initially used for characterizing some professionals who insistently reported possible threats to customers' safety deriving from weaknesses or errors in an artefact's design. Later on, 'whistleblowing' entered the parlance as a way of describing the public exposure of episodes of corruption, frauds, or, more generally, the misuse of power.

The specific nature of whistleblowing consists in the involvement of persons who face a dilemma between being loyal to the organization for which they work and to their fellow members, on the one hand, and exposing some wrongdoing within that organization, on the other. To complicate the scenario, a recurrent feature of cases of whistleblowing is that reporting wrongdoing typically entails serious consequences both for the whistleblowers (and, sometimes, even their friends and families) and for their organization. Indeed, many whistleblowers become known to the public not so much for their fight against corruption, the promotion of corporate responsibility, or the enhancement of government accountability, as for the tragic personal consequences they suffer or the reputational damages they allegedly cause to their organization.

To get an immediate illustration of this state of affairs, let us consider two significant contemporary examples of whistleblowers: Edward Snowden, who publicly revealed details of secret mass-surveillance programmes of the US and British governments; and Chelsea Manning, who revealed to WikiLeaks classified information about the US military operations in Iraq and Afghanistan. Although the stories of less famous whistleblowers might be different from Snowden's and Manning's, these cases have attracted significant public attention and have become a point of reference for many scholarly works on whistleblowing.

Edward Snowden

Edward Snowden was a computer specialist working for the Central Intelligence Agency (CIA) first, and then working as a subcontractee for the National Security Agency (NSA). Because of his role and responsibilities, Snowden had access to privileged information concerning the specifics of the global surveillance network through which the American secret services monitor telecommunication systems around the world. These controls were somewhat known since the Cold War. However, no substantive evidence had ever been produced to demonstrate how the system actually works.

In the aftermath of the 9/11 terrorist attacks, the NSA intensified its global surveillance systems, ending up monitoring ordinary citizens who were unrelated to criminal organizations. Snowden developed the conviction that, in the name of national security, the US government was illegitimately violating the privacy of millions of Americans as well as that of unwitting foreign citizens.

Snowden tried, first, to share his qualms with co-workers, but nobody, however similarly concerned, was willing to risk their career and life to expose this fact. Other members of the NSA had raised similar issues before, but they all got dismissed and, in certain cases, were taken to court and charged with, among other things, espionage. Coming to the conclusion that the situation could not be changed from within the NSA, Snowden made contacts with journalists from the *Guardian* and the *Washington Post*, to inform them of a mass-surveillance system known as PRISM. He then flew to Hong Kong, where he finally met the journalists in person, thus revealing his identity, and disclosed the relevant classified documents (documents he had carefully edited to minimize the possible harm that might derive from their circulation).

In June 2013, Snowden was officially charged with violating the 1917 Espionage Act and with theft of government property, facing the possibility of lifetime imprisonment. Snowden currently lives in Russia, where President Putin has granted him temporary asylum.

Chelsea Manning

Bradley, now Chelsea, Manning was an American Marine. While stationed in Iraq as an intelligence analyst, Manning gained privileged access to classified information, some of which concerned crimes committed by US troops. Among other things, she found videos that showed unarmed civilians being shot and killed by American soldiers. Horrified by such gross violations of human rights, she decided to take action.

She collected information about war logs in Iraq and Afghanistan, cables from the US State Department, and reports about the condition of prisoners at Guantánamo Bay. Eventually, Manning managed to leak some 750,000 classified documents to WikiLeaks, the famous international nonprofit organization created by Julian Assange that publishes secret information and classified documents in the name of a fully transparent society.

In 2013, Manning was sentenced to thirty-five years in prison on several counts, including the violation of the 1917 Espionage Act and theft of government property. After President Obama commuted her sentence, Manning was released from prison in May 2017.

The Duty of Whistleblowing

Snowden and Manning have been celebrated as paradigmatic examples of whistleblowers – as virtuous individuals who heroically act in the name of justice at their own personal risk. No doubt there is much to say in favour of the personal sacrifice and the public service that both Snowden and Manning exemplify. But we would like to challenge this heroic portrait of the whistleblower by asking a more fundamental question: is whistleblowing best understood as an *individual act* of dissent, motivated by *personal* reasons of justice and integrity, or as an *organizational practice*, justified as a matter of duty by *public* reasons of justice and accountability?

If we define 'whistleblowing' with reference to Snowden and Manning, then whistleblowing could not possibly be viewed as a duty. While the moral assessment of Snowden's and Manning's actions has been the object of extensive debate – with some critics regarding them as socially and politically dangerous, if not treasonous – it is quite clear that, even for their supporters, what Snowden and Manning did exceeds the limits of ordinary morality. Snowden's and Manning's actions, that is, go well beyond what one ought, necessarily, to do. The sacrifice of one's own life, family, and personal freedom cannot be morally demanded of anyone, no matter what cause is served by their action.

Whistleblowing would thus fall in the realm of supererogatory acts: those actions that are good to perform but that cannot be morally required (because, *inter alia*, of the costs they imply for the agents). Indeed, we can quite safely assume that few people would actually have done what Snowden and Manning did. Snowden and Manning are generally not considered ordinary persons acting on their civic duties, but heroes (this is especially the case with Snowden). This explains the resonance their stories have had and their consideration as sources of inspiration for virtuous behaviour worldwide.

If this is the best possible interpretation of Snowden's and Manning's disclosures, the answer to our central question in this book seems quite immediate and straightforward: no, whistleblowing cannot possibly be a duty.

But this is not an answer on which we wish to rest our case. In fact, we think that to construe whistleblowing – exclusively, or even just primarily – as an individual heroic act impoverishes our normative understanding of this practice as a powerful tool to counteract organizational wrongdoings. As we have just seen, if we were to limit our understanding of whistleblowing in this way, we would be unable to make it a requirement for anyone; it would remain a permissible and laudable, but optional, act of personal morality. Therefore, its role as a matter of public ethics would be almost negligible and thus not quite interesting from the perspective of political theory. But this conclusion would fail to do justice to whistleblowing's potential.

To bring this potential out, we suggest a new way to look at whistleblowing: as an organizational duty embedded within the best practices of public accountability. In this sense, whistleblowing adds something important to ordinary duties and responsibilities. Political theories standardly presume a duty to obey general laws as well as the rules of an organization. Whistleblowing is not only a matter of formal rule-following: it indicates the report of violations of those laws and rules. Both Snowden and Manning had the duty to oversee intelligence activities and process sensitive information, but they were under no duty to check the specific content of such information or the way it was obtained. Did Snowden or Manning have a duty to blow the whistle even if no law or internal rule required them to do so?

Our question is not whether Snowden's and Manning's actions could be legally justified under current laws and regulations. Ours is a question of public ethics. It concerns the normative justification of a distinctive duty to report organizational wrongdoings. While relevant kinds of wrongdoing may occur in either private or public organizations, in this book we are primarily concerned with the latter. Our discussion should be seen, therefore, as a contribution to a non-ideal political theory of the public order aimed at identifying organizational and individual duties when faced with some publicly salient wrong.

Within this general framework, therefore, we will

submit a justification of a duty of whistleblowing within public institutions vis-à-vis cases of abuse of public power. The cases of Snowden and Manning may be seen in this light quite straightforwardly. These cases have a clear public relevance, which they share with such other cases of institutional wrongdoing as, for example, political corruption. These are cases of abuse of public power, which may undermine the quality of the institutions of a democratic society and of the relations between citizens within them.

By bringing a wrongdoing to light, a well-regulated practice of whistleblowing offers an important contribution to the public accountability of an organization. Therefore, as we will argue, whistleblowing can be justified as a matter of duty *qua* a corrective practice within a general normative theory of institutions, because it qualifies the individual and organizational moral demands attached to rule-governed organizational roles. In this sense, the book offers an original addition from the perspective of political theory to current normative studies of whistleblowing, which have mainly concentrated on corporate responsibility from the perspective of business ethics.

The study of whistleblowing has been central to legal theory for some time (e.g., labour and corporate law), economics (e.g., business management and administration), and business ethics. The study of this practice from the perspective of political theory is still underdeveloped. But this is a perspective from which important insights may derive, especially regarding the normative status of this practice in the public domain and its possible contribution to the promotion of justice and public accountability in non-ideal conditions. In particular, a central but underexplored question concerns whether and how whistleblowing is morally justifiable, and, if so, whether it is required or merely permissible. This is a significant question for political analysis in its own right, but it also has important bearing on the discussion of the extent to which whistleblowers ought to be protected or rewarded. This book aims at filling this lacuna.

One of the main challenges of this study is the lack of general criteria to distinguish permissible whistleblowing from required whistleblowing. Sometimes, reporting a wrongdoing is very demanding because the whistleblower faces potentially burdensome consequences, including retaliation, losing their job, and even death threats, as the cases of Snowden, Manning, and many less famous whistleblowers show. In these cases, it is difficult to justify anything like a perfect duty of whistleblowing, although to blow the whistle could remain a good and praiseworthy thing to do. Other times, the available evidence might not be enough to prove an alleged wrongdoing, thus most likely making whistleblowing ineffective. Even if blowing the whistle is the morally right thing to do in the circumstances, it could disrupt relations among co-workers and severely compromise the reputation of the organization, thus diminishing its general trustworthiness. Also, potential whistleblowers might act for questionable reasons – for example, the possibility of retaliating against an obnoxious boss – rather than out of a duty. Finally, they might be tempted by possible gains – for example, being rewarded with a part of the sum recovered from a bribe – rather than being moved by moral motives.

To what extent should the justification of whistleblowing be sensitive to either the personal or general consequences it may have? Can we justify a general duty of whistleblowing? If so, how should we conceptualize it? Could such a duty be legally enforced? What kind of protection should whistleblowers receive? How can we make this practice safe both for whistleblowers and for those who are the object of their revelations? Is the duty of whistleblowing necessarily in conflict with other persons' rights to privacy?

This book addresses these and other questions and, in so doing, offers both guidance to navigate the main theories of whistleblowing and its own novel contribution to a political theory of this practice.

Plan of the Book

The book is divided into three chapters.

Chapter 1 sets the stage for the discussion in the subsequent two chapters. We illustrate the main difficulties scholars face in defining whistleblowing, even though the term is commonly used in the public debate. We propose a working definition of whistleblowing, analyse it, and use it to discuss the various elements that qualify the cases of Snowden and Manning as instances of this practice.

Chapter 2 presents the main normative line of argument of the book. We begin by offering a critical review of some current prominent theories of whistleblowing. Then, on a (broadly deontological) view, we present whistleblowing as a practice that concerns the actions of a member of a legitimate organization who has privileged access to information concerning some kind of wrongdoing that occurs within that organization. We discuss and defend the claim that whistleblowing is justifiable as a duty because it is a specific instantiation of the general organizational-membership duty of public accountability. This specific duty, as we shall argue, applies when a member of an organization has privileged access to information concerning uses of entrusted power within her organization – uses that contradict that power's mandate. The duty is performed in order to restore the logic of public accountability that the alleged occurrence of that wrongful practice or behaviour has altered.

Chapter 3 qualifies the duty of whistleblowing as an organizational practice. We discuss the possible tensions between discharging this duty and other possible (personal and organizational) duties the potential whistleblower may have (e.g., of personal trust or public security). We argue that the way out of these and other possible critiques of the stringency of the duty to blow the whistle requires distinguishing two dimensions of the interpersonal relations that whistleblowing involves: a public and a personal one. The conflation of these two dimensions has the problem of leading to too quick a dismissal of the duty of whistleblowing, which is seen, as a consequence, as being supererogatory. While we should recognize that discharging the duty to blow the whistle on organizational wrongdoing might undermine some bonds of trust at the personal level (e.g., relations of friendship), this practice has the capacity to enhance the quality of public relations of accountability.

We conclude, with some qualifications, that whistleblowing is one of the corrective organizational practices that ought to be implemented to counteract such serious forms of wrongdoing as corruption, especially when they occur in the public sector and involve public officials.

1

Defining Whistleblowing

Introduction

In a basic sense, whistleblowing consists in the practice of reporting wrongdoings. The term entered the public debate in the late 1950s, but, despite the growing discussion of this practice in academic as well as non-academic circles, no definition is generally accepted.[1] Formulating a definition capable of being precise enough to serve the purposes of academic research and nuanced enough to encompass the many current usages of the term in the public debate is a challenge for a number of reasons.

First of all, 'whistleblowing' is a metaphor: like the referee who, literally, blows the whistle to stop the action when players commit a foul during a game, whistleblowers signal that something (potentially) wrong is occurring (Bok, 1980, p. 2). As with many other figures of speech, when the metaphor of whistleblowing is applied to a complex set of different actions, its literal meaning becomes vague and imprecise. Although it may actually be suggestive of the emotions involved in the practice – the imperative need to bring an illegal or hazardous behaviour to a halt – a metaphor of this sort is unfit for providing either a precise definition or an encompassing account of whistleblowing.

A second difficulty comes from the fact that the current usages of the term 'whistleblowing' neither extensionally refer to a coherent set of actions nor intentionally track a distinctive category in the realm of practical normativity under which all relevant actions can be subsumed. Unlike purely philosophical concepts, 'whistleblowing' has so far been used as a semantic placeholder for a set of similar (although not homogeneous) practices that typically involve someone's reporting an alleged wrongdoing to someone else.

Related to this conceptual point, a normative issue applies too. The moral appreciation, social approval, and general normative evaluation of this practice have varied across different historical, cultural, and social contexts.[2] When it entered the public debate, 'whistleblowing' was used by journalists to characterize the action of professionals reporting such hazards as weaknesses or errors in an artefact's design with the intent of preventing a threat to customers' safety (see, for example, De George, 1981). Nowadays, 'whistleblowing' has entered common parlance as a way of describing the public exposure of episodes of corruption, fraud, or general abuses of power. Across all these usages, the term has been characteristically laden with an ambivalent connotation, swinging between the appreciation for a heroic act of denunciation and the suspicion – if not the condemnation – of a revelation that entails a breach of confidentiality akin to espionage.

A third difficulty comes from the distinctively multidisciplinary attention whistleblowing has attracted. The study of whistleblowing has been central for quite some time in legal theory (e.g., labour and corporate law), economics (e.g., business management and administration), and business ethics. This variety of approaches has resulted in a plurality of definitions that are difficult to reconcile in one unified and systematic view.[3]

This difficulty emerges quite strikingly from a general survey of the main theories in the debate. Richard De George (1981, 2010), whose work is considered a benchmark in business ethics, takes whistleblowing as the action of disclosing information about the possible harm caused by a certain product. Sissela Bok (1980) extends De George's view to general revelations made in the public interest of a society and presents whistleblowing as a preventive measure.[4] Norman Bowie (1982, pp. 142–8) adds violation of human rights as a reason that motivates whistleblowing. More recently, as attention to whistleblowing has increased, scholars have tried to work out more nuanced definitions of this practice – notably, some have insisted on the central significance of information concerning illegalities and other serious wrongdoings voluntarily disclosed by the members of an organization.[5]

This plethora of accounts and evaluative stances has made it particularly difficult to pinpoint the conceptual and normative essence of whistleblowing and is responsible for a blurring of the lines between this practice and such other potentially troublesome activities as spying on, or informing on, somebody.[6]

To avoid losing content and meaning, our primary aim in this chapter is to propose a working definition of whistleblowing that meets the following desiderata: (a) it captures the many salient features of the specific way of reporting wrongdoings that this practice implies; (b) it is sufficiently robust to hold across different disciplines and current usages of the term; (c) it is sufficiently normatively thin to avoid including any moral or political judgement in the description of the practice.

Let us start from this general and minimal definition:

> WHISTLEBLOWING: the practice through which a member of a legitimate organization voluntarily reports some wrongdoing, allegedly occurring within that organization, with the intention that corrective action should be taken to address it.[7]

We now elaborate on the constitutive elements of this definition in detail. This elaboration will guide us through the famous cases of Edward Snowden and Chelsea Manning in the section after the next.

Six Elements of Whistleblowing

Our working definition of the practice of whistleblowing contains six main elements regarding (i) the action of reporting (either authorized or unauthorized); (ii) the agent of the report (the whistleblower); (iii) the locus where the relevant facts occur (an organization); (iv) the object of the report (the wrongdoing); (v) the addressee of the report (either internal or external to the organization); and (vi) the motivation of the report (the intention to initiate a corrective action). Let us review each of these elements in turn.

(i) The action

In a basic and straightforward sense, the practice of whistleblowing consists in an action of *reporting*. But not just any act of reporting is an instance of whistleblowing. How does this action specifically qualify?

First of all, whistleblowing consists in a *voluntary* disclosure. This implies that a whistleblower does not typically act under duress – she is not revealing the occurrence of some wrongdoing under the threat or the use of force by a third party.[8] Whatever the justificatory grounds for reporting wrongdoings could possibly be, whistleblowing is not usually driven by the need to overcome the risk of physical force or psychological and social pressure.

Different commentators have pointed out different features of this voluntary act of reporting, concerning, for instance, its anonymity. We wish to be quite inclusive in our account, and, therefore, we recognize that the action of blowing the

22

whistle could take the form of either an open or an anonymous report, depending on the specific environmental circumstances in which it occurs. *Open* reports are usually considered an act of indictment – that is, a manifest accusation of some wrongdoing (see Jubb, 1999). *Anonymous* reports, instead, are similar to 'tips' (pieces of information, typically given in a confidential way) or 'leaks' (the intentional disclosure of secret information).[9]

In addition, we can distinguish between authorized and unauthorized reports, depending on the current legislation and local norms. Reports filed through *authorized* forms of whistleblowing are presented through legally or otherwise established organizational procedures. *Unauthorized* disclosures, like tips and leaks, are typically unlawful activities (e.g., when confidential pieces of information are reported to the press). Independently of their formal legal status, all actions of whistleblowing can be ethically problematic, as we shall see in chapter 3.

(ii) The agent

The second element to consider is the agent who blows the whistle. A whistleblower is a *member* of the organization in which the reported facts occur. So not just anyone who files a report on some questionable organizational practices or individual behaviour counts as a whistleblower. The report characteristically comes from the inside (Miceli and Near, 1992; Miceli et al., 2014).[10]

To be a member of an organization means to occupy a role within it, or, to put it differently, to perform a formal and regulated function that is coordinated with those assigned to other members. In this sense, possible whistleblowers include a company's employees, the officer of a public institution, a volunteer in a charity organization, and so on. Membership is not necessarily permanent; those who take part in the formal activities of an organization for a limited period of time may also qualify as whistleblowers. This could be the case with temporary workers or members of another organization currently working within the organization in which the relevant facts occur (these may be either subcontractors or consultants).

Not quite as straightforward a matter is whether both present and past members of an organization qualify. In the comprehensive spirit of our definition, we wish to include both kinds of members. However, when specific cases are under scrutiny, the temporal proximity or distance from the relevant facts may make a difference for assessing the whistleblower's action (depending, for example, on the reasons why the agent has decided to defer her report).

In either case, this membership requirement is crucial to distinguish the practice of whistleblowing as a particular way of reporting, irreducible to other frequently debated practices. This feature marks the difference, for example, between a whistleblower and either a 'spy' or a 'rat'. A spy is someone who collects information on the activities and plans of an enemy or competitor and keeps her action secretive. A whistleblower does not necessarily act secretly and does not necessarily try to obtain an advantage over, or discredit, somebody. The word 'rat', on the other hand, is an informal expression used to identify a despicable person who has been disloyal, betraying someone's trust and confidence. Although many whistleblowers have been accused of violating personal trust and organizational loyalty, their actions – as we shall see – are not typically (let alone necessarily) strategic.

Another feature of the agent is the position she has with respect to the piece of information which she has access to and then discloses. To put it crudely, a whistleblower is a person who, in virtue of the role she occupies within an organization, finds herself at the right place and time to gather relevant pieces of information about the questionable facts she reports. This is the sense in which we say that the whistleblower has *privileged* access to information. Relevant pieces of information may concern either the procedures of an organization or the behaviour of (some of) its members. As we shall see, the kind of information to which whistleblowers have access has been widely debated as an important piece of the justification of their action, as it provides the evidence for the report.

(iii) The locus

We have said that whistleblowing consists in the practice of reporting performed by a member of an organization, which is both the locus where the whistleblower acquires the information about the facts she reports and where those facts occur.

Essentially, according to a standard account in institutional theory, an organization is an embodied structure of interdependent roles or, more simply put, a structured body of people (see Miller, 2014). This essential characterization applies to private and public, governmental and nongovernmental organizations, and it includes such an array of instances as companies, corporations, and associations, and such institutions as banks and state offices. In our view, organizations do not necessarily have a particular shared purpose – such as a religious, educational, social, or political aim – but they are defined by their performing certain functions that qualify what their members do collectively.

Organizations are structured according to a statute or an internal code of conduct that establishes members with a set of rights and duties in accordance with each role they occupy and in keeping with a specific set of rules that assigns powers to each of these roles with a specific mandate. These rules are public in the sense that they are generally known and accessible to each and every member at all levels of the organization.[11] In this sense, we can refine our account of an organization as an embodied structure of interdependent roles governed by public rules.

An organization is legitimate when it is entitled (legally or morally) to the power it exercises through the actions of its members. To qualify relevant organizations as legitimate in a very broad sense is primarily necessary to distinguish whistleblowers from informants, who report, for example, on such criminal (and, therefore, illegitimate) organizations as the mafia. In our discussion, we align with the canon in the debate and assume without any further argument the legitimacy of the organizations in which the relevant reporting practices occur (see Davis, 1996).

Based on this characterization of the agents and locus of whistleblowing, we can also distinguish this practice from the less specific practice of bell ringing: the actions of conscientious citizens who report crimes and misdemeanours (see Miceli et al., 2014).[12] The practice of bell ringing is based on the idea of active and participatory citizenship, regardless of the agent's belonging to the specific organization in which the questionable facts occur.

(iv) The object

With these specifications of the formal aspects of whistleblowing on the table, we can now address the fourth substantive element that characterizes this practice: the object of the report. Per our definition, whistleblowing is the action of reporting some alleged *organizational wrongdoing* by a member of the organization.

This construal offers a first general qualification of the object of whistleblowing: a wrongful fact that occurs *within* an organization and is related to the uses of power associated with the roles performed by its members. Relevant facts may concern either a more or less systematic organizational practice (for example, clientelism as a practice to manage public calls for tenders) or an individual, more or less occasional, behaviour (for example, a manager's

28

misappropriation of company funds). The constant across these cases is an arbitrary deviation from the mandate with which either certain rule-based practices should occur or certain members should perform their role within the organization.

While we are making progress towards specifying the object of whistleblowing, we are still referring to a fairly encompassing account of wrongdoing that may include a large sample of objectionable or hazardous instances. We can take a further step and distinguish between two main kinds of instances. On the one hand, whistleblowers may report some *illegal* organizational practice or individual behaviour. This kind of wrongdoing may stem from either unlawful activities (for example, embezzlement) or illicit actions, such as the violations of organizational standards (like a dangerous error in an artefact's design). The wrongfulness of such instances can be established with reference either to the law or to an organization's internal norms. In any case, the alleged wrongdoing implies the violation of some formal rule.

A vast proportion of cases of whistleblowing concerns illegal actions of this sort. However, whistleblowing could also be about instances of *immorality* – that is, actions that, although not necessarily either unlawful or in contradiction with the letter of a rule, are nevertheless either contrary to the spirit of the rule or not permissible from a moral point of view. For example, an organization might not have a written policy about sexual harassment, and the current legislation may be vague about what counts as a criminal offence in this case. Nevertheless, to receive unwelcome sexual advances from a colleague is morally problematic, and may be the object of a whistleblower's report.

Depending on the kind of organization we consider, relevant institutional wrongdoings may vary in magnitude. For example, the report might concern large-scale violations of personal rights (as in the cases of Snowden and Manning that we revisit below) or petty abuses of power in a local small to medium-sized enterprise (as is the case in the examples we introduce later, of a bank and a hospital). Our account of whistleblowing is sufficiently flexible to encompass both scales of wrongdoing, as we will illustrate by discussing cases of different magnitudes at different places in the book.

Some accounts of whistleblowing have also embedded in the definition of the wrongdoing that is the object of this practice an admittedly vague criterion concerning its 'seriousness' (De George, 2010). Given our commitment to offering a description of whistleblowing, which is clearly separate from its normative evaluation and justification, we have dropped this requirement entirely.

The same reason of conceptual parsimony lies at the basis of our decision not to apply any specific epistemic standard to qualify the object of the report. Unlike other commentators, we have not incorporated in our definition any requirement concerning the standards of evidence that qualify the agent's knowledge of the wrongdoing she reports.[13] Rather, we refer to 'alleged wrongdoing'. We revisit the discussion of epistemic standards in the next chapter.

(v) The addressee

Since the constitutive action of whistleblowing is a report, our account of whistleblowing, as with that of any form of communication, requires us to characterize the report's addressee.[14] The relevant distinction here is between addressees that are either internal or external to the organization in which the alleged wrongdoing occurs.[15]

Internal whistleblowing could consist in the communication to a direct superior, to higher levels of management, or to a dedicated office appointed to investigate this kind of disclosure (such as, for instance, ombudsmen or ethical officers). Some organizations have implemented different channels to collect whistleblowers' reports, such as dedicated letter boxes and hotlines, and digital solutions such as emails and portals. *External* whistleblowing, on the other hand, involves reporting relevant information to such external entities as the police or the media or a governmental authority that has the power but not the knowledge to stop or prevent some wrongful action.

While internal whistleblowing is usually thought of as one of the best practices to oversee the uses of power within a legitimate organization, external whistleblowing has been standardly presented as an exceptional measure that usually follows the failure of internal whistleblowing. For the time being, we wish not to take a side in this debate, but refer to both kinds of whistleblowing as identifying possible addressees of this practice. We revisit this distinction for a normative evaluation in chapter 3.

(vi) The motivation

The final element we would like to qualify concerns the whistleblower's motivations. In a very basic sense, we can say that, in cases of whistleblowing, a member of an organization reports some alleged organizational wrongdoing in order to urge that *corrective action* be taken either to prevent that wrongdoing from occurring or to stop it.

While this motivation holds in these general terms, it is hard to offer more detail concerning the actual motivations underpinning any individual instance of whistleblowing. Whistleblowing has often been presented as a pro-social practice whose aim is the promotion of justice and moral rectitude within an organization and the welfare of its members (see Miceli and Near, 1992, pp. 28–30). However, the question of the real motivation – the set of individual psychological states and attitudes – behind the decision of a whistleblower to report a wrongdoing is a rather complex one that cannot be settled on a solid basis within a *political* theory of this practice.

As cases of whistleblowing often present themselves, we can see that they are typically motivated by ethical considerations. But this recurrent factual feature does not automatically preclude that a whistleblower may act with malice, or guarantee that her actions are totally independent from expectations of future rewards – such as, for example, a sum of the money recovered thanks to her blowing the whistle on a financial fraud or a case of embezzlement.[16] We cannot even exclude by hypothesis the possibility that a whistleblower acts on the desire to take revenge against a mean manager or an obnoxious colleague.

Whether selfish or altruistic, the whistleblower's actual psychological motivations seem of little significance within a political theory of whistleblowing, whose main aim is to offer a characterization (and, subsequently, a justification) of the public function of this practice. From this point of view, we think it is sufficient to characterize the whistleblowers' motivations in terms of a commitment to bringing about a positive change of the status quo by urging that corrective action be taken to address (prevent or stop) an alleged organizational wrongdoing.

The six elements can be summarized as in Table 1.

Having thus laid out the six constitutive elements of our working definition of whistleblowing, we can add flesh to the bones of this analysis by using it to discuss how the famous cases of Edward Snowden and Chelsea Manning qualify as instances of this practice.

The Cases of Snowden and Manning as Instances of Whistleblowing

As anticipated, the cases of Edward Snowden and Chelsea Manning are standardly referred to as paradigmatic instances of whistleblowing, in the scholarly and public debates alike. In light of the

Table 1 The constitutive elements of whistleblowing

Action: Report	Voluntary	Open/ anonymous	Legitimate/ unauthorized
Agent: Member of an organization	Privileged access to nonpublic information	Permanent/ temporary	Current/ former
Locus: Legitimate organization	Public	Private	Private
Object: Organizational Wrongdoing	Systematic/ occasional	Unlawful/ illicit/immoral practice or behaviour	Unlawful/ illicit/immoral practice or behaviour
Addressee: Internal	Supervisor	Higher management	
External			Police/Media agency
Motivation:	Altruistic	Altruistic	Selfish

conceptual analysis of whistleblowing presented in the previous section, we are now in a position to probe the extent to which they can actually perform this illustrative function. With an analytical working definition and its concrete illustration on the table, we shall then be in a position to proceed to the discussion of the normative status of whistleblowing, and its justification, in the next chapter.

Snowden

Recall that Edward Snowden is the CIA computer specialist who disclosed to the press the details of the mass-surveillance programmes put in place by the US and British governments.[17]

How exactly does Snowden's leak qualify as an instance of whistleblowing? To start, let us consider Snowden's action. To be sure, Snowden's revelation to the media qualifies as a voluntary report that took the form of an open disclosure of classified documents. This is a clear case of an unauthorized report: Snowden was in fact legally bound, in virtue of the mandate of his job, by a nondisclosure agreement.

As to Snowden himself as an agent – interestingly, and perhaps less straightforwardly – his job at the time of the report qualifies him as a whistleblower rather than just a bell ringer. While Snowden was not anymore an employee of the CIA, he was a current member of a private company (Dell Inc.) that was the contractor for another governmental organization (the NSA), to which Snowden was temporarily assigned as a computer specialist. While Snowden was not anymore a member of one of the loci where the facts he reported occurred (the CIA), nor was he a permanent member of the other locus (the NSA), in virtue of his job he still counts as a (temporary) member of the latter organization, per our definition. What is more, his job as a computer analyst gained him privileged access to the information (withheld from the public) necessary to gather the evidence that substantiated his report.

The evidence Snowden reported to the press makes evaluating the object of his report an immediately relevant matter of whistleblowing. The reported facts constitute an organizational wrongdoing as they refer to the systematic practice by the US and allied governments of listening to the personal phone calls of unwitting individuals, or reading their emails. This practice is allegedly wrong because, quite simply, it amounts to a systematic, coercively imposed violation of the fundamental liberal-democratic right to privacy. Therefore, regardless of its arguable legal status (such surveillance systems were authorized by the relevant governments), this practice is quite clearly problematic from a moral point of view as it occurred in patent violation of a fundamental individual moral right. (Note also that the legal status of the practice is itself quite unclear from the perspective of international regulations.)

Snowden's report had a troubled life as concerns its addressee. While ultimately the information about the relevant organizational wrongdoing was leaked to the press, Snowden did try to take the internal route first. When it became clear that his attempt at sharing his concerns with his colleagues was leading nowhere, he took the external route and disclosed his report to the press.

The decision to go public can be understood in light of Snowden's motivation to take action (and urge that others take action) to change a morally problematic status quo, in virtue of which the rights of many citizens worldwide were being unwarrantedly violated. His decision to flee his job and his country and go public with his report reveals his altruistic motives; the costs he had to endure as a consequence of his report (including the prospect of lifetime imprisonment) run counter to any reasonable self-regarding motivation.

Manning

Chelsea Manning's case is quite straightforward: an American Marine stationed in Iraq brought to the public attention some gross violations of human rights perpetrated by the US military in Iraq and Afghanistan, by disclosing classified information that she came to know of in her capacity as an intelligence analyst.[18] Let us briefly run this case through our six definitional elements of whistleblowing.

As in Snowden's case, Manning's action no doubt qualifies as a voluntary, open, and unauthorized report of classified information she was under a legal obligation not to disclose. Unlike Snowden, when Manning took this action, she was a current and permanent member of the US Marine Corps, a part of the public legitimate organization (the US Army) within which the contested facts had occurred. It was in virtue of her role as an intelligence analyst that Manning came to know about those facts and to know she could have privileged access to the classified documents (including war logs in Iraq and Afghanistan, cables from the US State Department, and reports about the prisoners' conditions at Guantánamo), which constituted the nonpublic evidence on which her report was subsequently based. So Manning's case also provides an upfront illustration of what the agent and the locus of whistleblowing paradigmatically are.

Like Snowden's report, Manning's was meant to urge that action be taken to change a status quo threatening the life of many innocent individuals. In her case, too, this justice-driven motivation, as well as the negative personal consequences she had to face (recall that Manning received a court-martial conviction), reveals the altruistic rationale of the action.

In particular, Manning's disclosure regarded gross violation of human rights on the part of the US Army. These included the murder of unarmed civilians (e.g., the Granai airstrike in Afghanistan), as well as the brutal treatment of detainees and the arbitrary detention of civilians (which was revealed, e.g., in the Guantánamo Bay files).[19] There is little doubt, therefore, that its object concerned the allegation of wrongful practices and behaviours that were both systemic (e.g., the prisoners' treatment) and occasional (e.g., the airstrikes). While the legality of some of the reported military operations has been a matter of debate (e.g., the 12 July 2007 Baghdad airstrike), all relevant facts raise serious moral concerns insofar as they constitute an alleged violation of such individual fundamental moral rights as those to life, security, and bodily integrity. However, we should add that not all the classified documents Manning disclosed, through WikiLeaks or otherwise, contained information exclusively relevant to this main object of moral concern (consider, e.g., the documents made accessible through so-called Cablegate).[20] No editing of the relevant files was undertaken to circumscribe their impact and possible consequences (e.g., for national security). While this aspect does not undermine the plausibility of placing Manning's case under the description of an act of whistleblowing, it may have an impact on the normative assessment of the case. We shall revisit this point later.

Similar considerations apply to the vicissitudes that led Manning to go public and reveal via WikiLeaks the documents to which she had access. Unlike Snowden, Manning leaked the various files she managed to collect without first trying to address her concerns either to other fellow members of the Marine Corps or to her direct superiors. The addressee of Manning's report is entirely external. These differences granted, both Manning's and Snowden's cases satisfy the essential elements of whistleblowing, per our analytical characterization, and therefore qualify as illustrative instances of this practice.

Conclusion

Our analytical endeavour in this chapter has aimed to clarify what it is like to be a whistleblower. We have also shown, with the aid of our analytical definition, the exact sense in which the two cases of Edward Snowden and Chelsea Manning have rightly attracted scholarly and public interest as instances of whistleblowing.

But there is more to it. In fact, our conceptual analysis can also be fruitfully employed to dispel possible inappropriate references to this practice to indicate any kind of report of some wrongdoing. The distinctive feature of philosophical definitions (unlike general, more or less suggestive, characterizations) is that they provide a set of individually necessary but only jointly sufficient conditions to describe certain states of affairs in a given manner by calling them specific names. None of the six constitutive elements of whistleblowing we have identified, discussed, and illustrated (nor a combination of some of those) is, therefore, sufficient to qualify a certain act of disclosure as an instance of whistleblowing proper. We can speak of whistleblowing only when we can tick all six boxes (some of whose variants we have summarized in table 1).

As seen, this set of conditions is fully satisfied as concerns Snowden's and Manning's disclosures. Conversely, the test can rule out such cases as that of a police officer who reveals the details of some undercover operation to narco-traffickers under investigation in exchange for a share of their profits, because neither the object of his disclosure nor his motivation would qualify. But our test is also helpful to identify some not-so-obvious false positives.

Consider the case of Erin Brockovich, a law clerk who discovered in the early nineties that the cause of a series of illnesses in the town of Hinckley, California, was the presence of hexavalent chromium in wastewater from a Pacific Gas & Electric (PG&E) plant.[21] Surely enough, many of the constitutive elements of whistleblowing are verified in this case: Brockovich took legal action to report her findings against PG&E in order to terminate (and seek compensation for the damages deriving from) this private company's practices of chemical-waste disposal, which were posing a serious threat to the fundamental right to health of many unsuspecting citizens. Nevertheless, Brockovich is not a whistleblower, because she was neither a current nor a previous PG&E employee. Failing the element of membership in the organization where the reported wrong had occurred, Brockovich, as an agent, does not meet one of the necessary conditions for being considered a whistleblower (perhaps her case is that of a bell ringer), although her action can be equally applauded in the name of justice and solidarity.

Another popular but analogously misplaced reference to the conceptual category of whistleblowing concerns the case of Julian Assange. Assange is a skilful hacker who, in 2006, founded WikiLeaks, a 'multi-national media organization and associated library' whose aim is to publish 'large datasets of censored or otherwise restricted official materials involving war, spying and corruption', with the goal 'to bring important news and information to the public' (WikiLeaks, 2011). Assange has frequently been presented as a whistleblower. His name is quite rightly associated with cases of whistleblowing; for example, WikiLeaks was the channel through which Manning circulated her evidence of the US military abuses. However, our analysis suggests Assange himself cannot be considered a whistleblower. While WikiLeaks has played an important role in exposing to the public relevant cases of organizational wrongdoing, Assange's action has always come from the outside of the organizations in which the reported wrongs occurred. He has never acquired the pieces of information he revealed because of his privileged position as a member of a defective organization; he has, rather, been the addressee of such information (as was the case with Manning). Assange's role is more akin to that of an investigative journalist. Sometimes, journalists report the same kinds of organizational wrongdoing as whistleblowers report. But would we ever characterize such a journalist as a whistleblower?

That seems quite inappropriate. Surely, a journalist may make whistleblowing possible by receiving and disclosing the whistleblower's report, and so may Assange. However, in that case, because she is not the source of the relevant information, a journalist is not a whistleblower herself.[22]

These conceptual clarifications are necessary in order to have a clear grasp of the kind of practice in which whistleblowing consists. Besides incarnating a paramount philosophical virtue, this clarification is necessary to focus with precision the object of a political theory of whistleblowing that is capable of making specific sense of the status of this practice and the role it could play within a general normative characterization of what public ethics requires in non-ideal conditions.[23]

To elaborate such a theory, an accurate normative discussion concerning the justification of whistleblowing is required to supplement the analytical description we have just provided. This is our task for the next chapter.

2

The Practice of Whistleblowing as a Duty

Introduction

As detailed in the previous chapter, by 'whistle-blowing' we indicate the practice through which the member of a legitimate organization voluntarily reports some wrongdoing, allegedly occurring within that organization, with the intention that corrective action should be taken to address it. In this chapter, we clarify the basic sense in which whistleblowing is a specific organizational reporting practice that should be implemented as a matter of duty. By 'organization', we mean a system of embodied, interdependent, rule-governed roles. We argue that the duty to blow the whistle on organizational wrongdoing is justified when facing either some practice within an organization, or the behaviour of some of its members, that contradicts the mandate with which power is attributed to any such role.

This justification, as presented in this chapter, applies to whistleblowing generally. However, given the specific focus of this book, we are particularly interested in developing the normative import of our argument as concerns wrongdoing in public institutions. This will be done in chapter 3.

Our conceptual analysis so far has offered grounds for ascertaining what acts of disclosure should be couched in the parlance of whistleblowing. This is important, we have argued, in order to offer simultaneously an accurate technical description of a well-circumscribed class of actions and make sense of current common usages of the term. As shown, while our analytical test is capable of tracking down some glaring false positives (such as the cases of Erin Brockovich and Julian Assange), it has reinforced the fittingness of the widespread references to Edward Snowden's and Chelsea Manning's disclosures as paradigmatic instances of whistleblowing.

As seen, Snowden's and Manning's cases present all the necessary elements of whistleblowing (concerning the relevant kind of actions, agents, locus, object, addressee and motivation). They also share another striking feature. Snowden's and Manning's deliberate decisions to report rested on high moral grounds. They forwent their lives, families, friends and careers to do something good; they exposed organizational wrongdoings threatening the fundamental rights and liberties of other individuals.

However, if what Snowden and Manning did was morally good, one might wonder whether any other member of the NSA or the US Marine Corps could or should have reported such wrongdoings. Did Snowden and Manning have exclusive access to the information they eventually disclosed? Or were fellow members of their respective organizations in either the same or a significantly analogous position? Would others who found themselves in their shoes have done the same? And if others could have done the same, were they duty-bound to do so?

Reading the details of their stories, many would probably think that what Snowden and Manning did goes well beyond what most people would do if they were in a similar position. The depth and breadth of the risks they undertook and the tragic personal consequences they suffered offer good enough ground to hypothesize that, although Snowden's and Manning's actions are morally praiseworthy, what they did goes beyond their – or in fact anyone else's – call of duty. Snowden's disclosure was morally good, but his colleagues who decided not to join him did nothing wrong, all things considered.

If we were to derive justifying reasons for blowing the whistle from Snowden's and Manning's vicissitudes, we would have to go beyond the boundaries of what ordinary morality requires. Differently put, what Snowden and Manning (and many other whistleblowers) did exceeds the standards of what one ought necessarily to do. Their actions fall, rather, into the realm of the supererogatory: they were morally good actions that no one in either Snowden's or Manning's position ought necessarily to do in standard conditions.

This view of whistleblowing as the heroic endeavour of David against Goliath is quite common in the current academic debate, as well as the public debate.[1] But to see whistleblowing as a supererogation has the effect of reducing any such report of organizational wrongdoing to a one-shot game in which an individual sacrifices her life and career for the sake of higher moral ideals and goals. If whistleblowing were supererogatory in this sense, whistleblowers would be heroes and their actions would be extraordinary and praiseworthy; but no general moral 'ought' or principle of justice could possibly fit the profile of a hero.

So if, based on the lessons learnt from our

two epitomic instances of whistleblowing, supererogation were to offer the best possible philosophical framing for thinking about the justification of whistleblowing, the question of the normative status of this practice would translate into the terms of what is morally permissible to an agent as a question of personal ethics (the set of moral norms and commitments that regulate individual personal behaviour). No normative ground would be available to think about the justification of whistleblowing in terms of a set of actions morally required of an agent as a question of public ethics. But these are the terms that matter from the perspective of political theory. From this perspective, the question concerning the normative status of whistleblowing is not about the justification of an individual response to an emergency. Rather, it regards the justification of a practice: a standard procedure within legitimate organizations. This perspective allows focalizing, *inter alia*, upon the duties that ought to guide someone's action in virtue of the role she occupies within an organization (and not because of the specific individual she is, or the personal qualities she has).

Therefore, the relevant question for political theorists is not what, say, Snowden and Manning ought to do because of the *specific persons* they are; nor is it whether their disclosures were permissible, *qua* morally good actions, in virtue of the *particular professional tasks* they had within their respective organizations. The question is what is generally morally required, as a practice, of *anyone* (Snowden and Manning included) who had privileged access to some information concerning some kind of wrongdoing allegedly happening within the organization of which she is a member. This is the distinct sense in which we ask the question of whether whistleblowing is a duty.

The question of the public function of whistleblowing as a matter of public, rather than either personal or professional, ethics has been surprisingly neglected in the otherwise growing normative discussion of this practice. Most commentators have, in fact, engaged with the justification of this practice as something a member of a legitimate organization *may* – but not necessarily *ought* to – do in standard conditions. Even those who have inquired into whether the members of a legitimate organization have a duty to report wrongdoings, as we shall see, have made it a very limited conditional duty (see, e.g., Boot, 2017).

Some have suggested that only legal norms or an otherwise enforceable organizational code of professional conduct could justify a duty of whistleblowing as a practice (Leys and Vandekerckhove, 2014; Tsahuridu and Vandekerckhove, 2008; Vandekerckhove and Tsahuridu, 2010). For physicians, lawyers, or engineers, for example, reporting cases of malpractice is often part of their formal specific professional obligations. If we considered only these cases, the question of whether whistleblowing is a duty would not require much in terms of moral reasoning. Consequently, the normative strength and cogency of such a duty would derive from a general obligation to comply with existing formal norms (Raz, 1979, pp. 3–36). If whistleblowing were a legal duty in this sense, its normative status would be entirely third-personal. The cogency of this duty would derive from the coercive imposition and threats of sanctions. In this sense, whistleblowing would not count as a voluntary act of reporting (as per its definition) that responds to a specific demand of public ethics.

From this, it follows that the question of whether whistleblowing is a duty becomes normatively interesting to the extent that it is capable of capturing a distinctive set of moral demands. The challenge is to explore the normative space for justifying such a set of moral demands that makes the organizational practice of whistleblowing a duty – something the members of a legitimate organization ought necessarily to do (in standard conditions) even when no law or other legally enforceable rule requires it.

Whistleblowing as a Duty: Two Current Received Views

As we have anticipated, the question of whether whistleblowing is a duty has received little scrutiny. In the current normative debate, two main received views are available: a harm-based view and a complicity-based view.

Of the six main definitional elements of whistleblowing we have identified, these views diverge only in their normative interpretation of the object of the report, on which the two justificatory stories for conceiving whistleblowing as a moral 'ought' ultimately depend. The harm-based view and the complicity-based view share the idea that the object of the report must be some kind of *serious wrong*. The normative qualification that the occurred wrongdoing is 'serious' is meant to fix a threshold below which the facts under scrutiny do not give the agent a sufficient reason to blow the whistle. Granted this similarity, on the former view whistleblowing is a duty insofar as this practice is necessary to stop or prevent some harm, while on the latter view its moral status derives from the necessity to avoid complicity in wrongdoing.

The occurrence of a harmful wrong and the relative position of the potential whistleblower with respect to it provide normative reasons to report the relevant wrongdoing as a matter of duty. The stringency of such a duty – that is, whether whistleblowing ought to be done necessarily, or only possibly – varies according to the evidence that supports the report and the consequences the potential whistleblower could face. Let us take a closer look at these distinguishing aspects of the received views in turn.

Harm-based views

One of the major accounts of the duty of whistleblowing comes from a consequentialist perspective and may be summarized thus:

THE HARM-BASED VIEW OF WHISTLEBLOWING: a member of an organization ought to blow the whistle when doing so may prevent or stop a serious harm stemming from some behaviour or practices of that organization, about which she has documented evidence, at a reasonable cost to herself.

This statement of the harm-based view is a generalization of De George's (2010) and Bowie's (1982) arguments, which have had a wide resonance in the fields of business ethics and corporate social responsibility.

On the harm-based view, the duty to blow the whistle is triggered when a serious harm occurs. This kind of harm includes those wrongdoings that cause some measurable damage to people's health and welfare (from psychological discomfort to physical impairment), possible environmental hazards, and such behaviours contrary to the public interest as fraud and corruption (Kumar and Santoro, 2017). The qualification of this kind of harm's being 'serious' is meant to establish a threshold, which should discriminate between reports that pinpoint actual damages to individuals and society and those that present trivial complaints (for example, concerning either petty offences among colleagues or the unwelcome demands of a bossy superior).

The normative stringency of this duty is determined by two factors: the available evidence of the (actual or potential) occurrence of a relevant kind of harm, and the costs associated with reporting it. If a whistleblower is unable to corroborate her accusation with substantive evidence, her report is morally permissible but not required. De George

(2010, p. 302), for example, sets this standard of evidence as having proof that could convince an impartial observer. But sufficiently robust evidence might not justify whistleblowing as a matter of duty if discharging this duty comes at an unreasonable cost for the whistleblower. To assess this cost, the possible negative personal consequences that may result from the whistleblower's disclosure (e.g., risks of retaliation) should not outweigh the whistleblower's expectation concerning the efficacy of their disclosure to bring about some significantly positive change to the status quo.

Many commentators have been critical of the harm-based view on a number of different counts (see, *inter alia*, Davis, 1996, pp. 8–10; Hoffman and Schwartz, 2015). Two of these critiques are particularly relevant to our discussion.

First, harm-based views require too high a standard of evidence for identifying relevant wrongdoings. How many members of an organization can be plausibly thought to have the capacity of searching for and producing documented evidence – evidence sufficiently solid to convince an impartial observer – about the occurrence of any wrongdoing? Access to robust evidence of this kind might be available only to a very limited number of persons, typically occupying either managerial or technical positions. While this might have been the case with Snowden and Manning, we may well think of other cases where lower-level employees have grown a suspicion (to the best of their knowledge) that might be worth pursuing, but this approach risks excluding such cases. To wit, the harm-based view entails too narrow a characterization of the possible *agents* of whistleblowing.

Second, and more importantly, even if we set this epistemic problem aside, identifying relevant instances of wrongdoing with actions that generate some serious harm offers a very narrow account of the *object* of whistleblowing too. Some actions may be morally problematic although they do not produce any measurable harmful consequence in the terms that, for example, De George has hypothesized.

Imagine the case of a chief surgeon who works in a public hospital and governs the hiring practices of his ward according to nepotistic dynamics. Imagine further that the appointed doctors happen to be good surgeons and that luck has it that, because the ward is situated in an unappealing area, jobs there have not been greatly in demand. No serious harm seems obviously to derive from this practice: those who are hired are capable of doing their job, and no other candidates' aspirations have so far been frustrated. So, because no harm ensues, there is no way this case of nepotism can be detected from outside the ward and questioned, unless a member of the ward discloses it. Why is this a problem? Because there seems to be a sense in which allocating jobs in the public sector in virtue of someone's personal ties is morally objectionable in itself, even if the circumstances are such that no measurable harm is caused. If we adopted the harm-based view of whistleblowing, when this kind of harm is not present, no ward member who took issue with the alleged inherent wrongness of this practice would have a justified duty to blow the whistle. Therefore, an allegedly wrongful practice may continue undisturbed.

Complicity-based views

Cognizant of these limitations of the harm-based view, defenders of the complicity-based view try to offer a more inclusive justification of the duty of whistleblowing in deontological terms. A statement of the view, which generalizes Davis's (1996, 2003) and Brenkert's (2010) positions, is as follows:

> THE COMPLICITY-BASED VIEW OF WHISTLE-BLOWING: a member of an organization ought to blow the whistle when, first, she believes

58

doing so could avoid her complicity with the occurrence of some wrongful behaviour or practice within her organization and, second, her beliefs are justified and true.

Interestingly, in this view, the duty of whistleblowing is independent of the object of the report, whether it consists in a special class of wrongful actions or is causally related to the occurrence of some measurable kind of harm. Insofar as some kind of wrong has occurred (or is likely to occur) and the member of an organization is somehow related to its occurrence (if only because she is justifiably and truthfully aware of it), whistleblowing is justified. So, according to the complicity-based view, the ward member who is aware of the chief surgeon's nepotistic hiring practices ought to blow the whistle, even if luck has it that no measurable harm for any individual or the public interest has yet ensued from those practices. This duty derives from the whistleblower's commitment to avoiding complicity with something morally objectionable (whatever that is), provided that this commitment is supported by justified and true beliefs.

The complicity-based view scores quite well in terms of avoiding the narrowness of harm-based views. But this view has two main limits itself. First, the resort to an idea of complicity might be no less controversial than that to harm.[2] In a very basic sense, any complicity-based justification of whistleblowing should specify what being an accomplice in a wrongdoing means and entails – whether it involves, for example, either somebody's active participation in wrongdoing, or his encouragement or assistance in bringing something wrong about, or both. The ward member in our example could find himself mixed up in, or just become aware of, the chief surgeon's nepotistic hiring practices, while he did not contribute to setting them up. Therefore, he would not be playing any active or wilful role in the occurrence of the wrongdoing. His omitting to report might nevertheless condone the occurrence of a morally questionable practice. Does this make him a potential accomplice who has, therefore, a duty to blow the whistle on the chief surgeon? Depending on the normative view of complicity that we adopt, the duty of whistleblowing could significantly vary, but proponents of the complicity-based view have not been forthcoming on this point.

But let us assume that a generally acceptable normative account of complicity is available. A familiar epistemic problem (that we have already encountered with reference to the harm-based view) remains. In this case, the problem concerns the standard of evidence that substantiates the beliefs of the potential whistleblower. As seen, for example, Davis (1996, p. 11) adopts a twofold standard: the whistleblower's beliefs must be justified *and* true. Brought to bear on our example, this standard requires – in the first place – that the ward member acquires robust evidence about the chief surgeon's nepotistic practices and, therefore, that his beliefs are justified. This acquisition involves and presumes a deep understanding of the functioning of the hospital's structure and hiring system, on the basis of which his judgement could be safely grounded. As seen also with reference to the impartial observer's test at work in De George's harm-based position, this requirement is quite epistemically demanding and might be met only by a very limited number of people within an organization.

But there is more to the demandingness of the complicity-based view. Even if the potential whistleblower's beliefs were so grounded, this would be insufficient to justify his blowing the whistle as a matter of duty. His beliefs would also have to be true. A true belief is a belief whose propositional content is a fact – that is, something that is indisputably the case. This requirement raises the bar of epistemic demandingness even higher as it entails that one ought to blow the whistle only when something wrong is *actually* occurring. But is this standard of belief ever achieved? And, in fact, is it a standard of belief that can be justifiably demanded of anyone? The most common cases of whistle-blowing see people acting on reasonable suspicions – beliefs formed on specific and articulable facts, along with the rational inferences the people can formulate. This was the case, for example, with Manning, whose role as an intelligence analyst enabled her to gather and circulate troubling mate-rial (e.g., videos of unnamed people struck by US drones) that could subsequently be tested to estab-lish the truth of facts.

Whistleblowing as a Problem of Public Ethics

Both the harm- and complicity-based received views of whistleblowing offer a justification of this prac-tice as a matter of moral duty with reference to only a very limited number of cases. This limited scope is problematic, we have seen, because it rests on very controversial normative criteria (concerning the object of the report, on the harm-based view) and epistemic assumptions (concerning the standard of evidence required to uphold the report, on both views).

Taken together, these limitations result in the exclusion of otherwise interestingly objectionable cases of 'harmless' wrongdoings (as in the case of nepotism we have discussed above) and potentially relevant disclosures, based on the reasonable inferences and to-the-best-of-one's-knowledge suspicions of members of an organization with no special professional skills or technical competences.[3]

This latter point has also the disappointing implication of offering a justification of the duty of whistleblowing that is in fact parasitic on the specific responsibilities to report relevant misdemeanours that certain particular members of an organization may happen to have either in virtue of their specific managerial role or their professional competences.[4] In this sense, whistleblowing would not denote a specific practice that can be demanded as a matter of duty. It would only be a – possibly rhetorically attractive – way to indicate some professional duties that some (but not all) members of an organization have to watch over organizational malfunctioning.[5]

To avoid these unwarranted limitations, our defence of the duty of whistleblowing must meet four conditions. We should demonstrate that standard (not *ad personam*) conditions obtain when a member of a legitimate organization ought, necessarily, to report an alleged wrongdoing, even if:

(a) the relevant objectionable practice or behaviour does not apparently cause any measurable harm;

(b) the duty to report is not included in (nor can it be entirely reduced to) her ordinary professional responsibilities;

(c) she did not have any direct role either in executing the objectionable behaviour or in setting up the objectionable organizational practice; and

(d) no special cognitive skill or professional expertise is presupposed to appreciate, gather, and process the relevant information to uphold the report.

This is an admittedly stringent set of conditions. Nevertheless, we think it is a set worth adopting because, if we manage to show the duty of whistleblowing obtains in the cases that satisfy all the conditions in the set, then our justification holds *a fortiori* in all other cases when some but not all conditions are met.

To get our argument off the ground, we propose the following thought experiment:

> While you are at the bank, a robber storms in. You stand next to the exit door, and you realize that if you stick your foot out, you can make the robber trip on his way out, thus enabling his arrest by the bank's guard.

Ought you to stick out your foot? To make this scenario more stringent, imagine your intervention is effortless (you, but only you, are really well positioned) and that it is reasonable to presume that, if the robber is made to trip, he will lose his weapon and no one will predictably get hurt. Imagine further that you are not the bank guard or a cop and that you are just an ordinary customer, not connected to the bank in any professional capacity or personally to anyone else in the bank (the robber included) in any way. Do you have a moral duty to act?

Most people would agree that you do not. Of course, it would be good and praiseworthy if you did so; you would probably see your picture in the newspaper the following day as the local hero. But if you stood still, would anyone – within the bank or outside – be morally entitled to blame you?[6] We want to suggest that no one – within the bank or outside – could ask you why you did not act; no one could justifiably hold you accountable for your decision, and, even if someone asked you to explain your behaviour (e.g., during the police investigation), you should not justify yourself in a way that is significantly different from what anyone else in the bank is required or expected to do.

But let us complicate this scenario a little: what if, instead of an innocent bystander – but all other things being equal – you were one of the bank's employees? Would the fact that you are an employee – namely, a member of a legitimate organization – change, in a significant way, the situation? In particular, could your other colleagues or, in fact, the bank manager, who can see the privileged position you occupy, justifiably ask you to account for your decision not to try to stop the robber? A positive answer to this question does not strike us anymore as utterly implausible. While it might be too strong a conclusion to say you are blameworthy for your inaction, it does not seem unreasonable to think you owe an explanation for it (at least, and primarily) to your colleagues.

If you are prepared to entertain this consideration, then we are a step closer to seeing the working of our justificatory story. But let us make another thought experiment, which may take us even closer:

> As a bank clerk, you come to develop the reasonable belief (based on some rumours) that one of your colleagues is using customers' money to trade online. One day, while you stand next to his desk,

by peeking at his computer monitor, you realize
that if you call your supervisor at that very moment,
you can expose your colleague, thus enabling his
arrest in the act by the bank's guard.

Let us suppose no apparent measurable harm is
caused by your colleague's behaviour; he takes only
small amounts of money (say, one penny) from
several accounts, and he always returns the money
to its owners. As in the case above, imagine further
that your intervention is effortless (you, but only
you, are really well positioned) and that it is reasonable to presume that your supervisor will come
presently. Let us also posit that your job description does not ordinarily involve any supervisory
function of your colleagues' work and that you are
not personally related to your colleague or any of
his customers in any way. You are just at the right
time and place to take action against an inherently
objectionable behaviour, and if you fail to act in
that very moment, you have no reason to think your
colleague's alleged wrongdoing could otherwise be
discovered and stopped. Ought you to act?

We think you ought to act in this case. If you failed
to act, you could be held justifiably accountable to
provide an explanation to your other colleagues,
your superiors, and possibly external agents (e.g.,
legal authorities) of why you decided not to act.

But, undoubtedly, the interesting question is why you would have such a duty. What is its normative source?

Certainly, this duty does not derive from a general moral commitment to preventing a measurable harm (which is not implicated by assumption in this case), nor does it seem unequivocal that your fortuitous position on that day, close to your colleague's desk, makes you an accomplice of his misbehaviour. So, were we to resort to either of the received views concerning the justification of whistleblowing, we would not be able to make normative sense of our intuitive positive reaction to the question of whether you had a duty to expose your cunning colleague. Furthermore, we have already established that your duty to report may not derive from your professional responsibilities, because your job description does not include any task of supervision. Nor should we assume any special cognitive skill or professional expertise on your part; it is a matter of standard knowledge for a bank employee to recognize uses of customers' money of this sort as inherently objectionable (and, in fact, illegal too).

So, what is the normative difference between your position as a bank customer who witnesses a robbery, in the first scenario, and as a bank employee who witnesses a colleague's misappropriation of customers' money, in this latter elaboration? Failing the resort to the harm- and complicity-based explanations we have just reviewed, our suggestion is that this difference must be searched for in the distinctive set of role-based moral demands that a person acquires in virtue of her organizational membership. This is the crux of our argument, which we are now moving on to expound.

The Duty of Whistleblowing:
The Public-accountability-based View

How does organizational membership matter to the justification of the duty of whistleblowing? To address this crucial question, we must clarify what an organization is, and, especially, the specific nature of the structural relations its members entertain.

According to a well-established characterization in institutional theory, an organization is a system of interdependent embodied roles (the members' functions), governed by *public rules* to which *powers* are attached with a specific *mandate* (Bovens, 1998, pp. 9–20; Miller, 2014). Notably, the rules are *public* in the sense that they are generally known; the set of *powers* specifies the appropriate range of actions for each role, whose performance structurally depends on that of the other roles within the organization; and the *mandate* establishes the appropriate ways in which, and matters over which, such actions should be taken. So conceived, organizations generate a system of rights and correlative duties that people hold in virtue of their occupying specific interdependent roles within them. People have these rights and duties *because* they are the members of a legitimate organization; therefore, the normative structural relations between them are constituted by, and are not prior to, the existence of that organization. Our argument aims to show that this set of organizational duties includes the practice of whistleblowing. Let us see how.

To be sure, the terms of the mandate with which power is entrusted to each organizational role allow for some discretion. Nevertheless, there is a general expectation that those who occupy those roles do so in a way they can explain publicly with reference to the rationale (either the letter or the spirit) of the rule that governs their role (Ceva and Ferretti, 2014, p. 130). Thus, when people interact as members of an organization, their primary and essential mode of interaction is through relations of *accountability*. A member of an organization is accountable in the sense that she is expected to justify the actions she takes and the decisions she makes. Those who occupy a specific role are directly accountable to the other members of the same organization for the uses they make of the powers that come with their role; these uses must be made in keeping with the terms of the mandate established by the rules that govern those roles.[7]

These structural relations of accountability are mutual. The members of an organization are primarily accountable to one another for the uses they make of their entrusted power, rather than to a third-personal authority. Of course, the violation of certain rules may require the involvement of a third-party enforcing authority – for example, for attributing punishments. Nevertheless, given the interdependence of organizational roles, the primary authorities to whom a justification is owed for the uses one makes of one's entrusted role-associated power are the fellow members of the organization to which one belongs. In this sense, the structural relations between the members of an organization are *second-personal* (see Darwall, 2009; Feinberg, 1970). And the justification that those who entertain these relations owe to each other for the uses they make of the powers associated with their office is *public* in the sense that it must be generally recognizable as an appropriate reason for action in

71

keeping with the terms of the mandate with which that power was given to them in virtue of their role (Ceva and Bocchiola, forthcoming).

This characterization seems good enough to give a sense of how this idea of public accountability has more precise a referent than that of harm and of complicity that we reviewed in the previous section. We suggest resorting to this idea as a normative guidance for the justification of the duty of whistleblowing.

To see this, let us revisit our last thought experiment. One of your colleagues is using customers' money to trade online. In that action, he uses the power he has as an employee of the bank, the organization to which you both belong. But he is also pursuing an agenda (self-enrichment) that is alien to that of the bank and its customers, and – ultimately, and most significantly – that contradicts the terms of the mandate that governs the role that gives him the power to act in that very moment. Now, as seen, because of his organizational membership and the capacity in which he is acting, your cunning colleague has a second-personal duty to account for the uses he makes of his power – the capacity to access customers' accounts and manage their money – publicly. But this kind of justification is not available for his behaviour, because the rationale of the agenda he pursues contradicts the terms of the mandate with which his power was attributed to the role he occupies and ought, therefore, to be exercised.

This is the sense in which, we argue, your cunning colleague's behaviour is objectionable in itself. What is more, we contend that his behaviour is objectionable in the sense of being *inherently* wrong because, in executing it, your colleague fails to act on the duty of public accountability that is binding on him in virtue of his organizational membership. Your cunning colleague's behaviour is objectionable even though it does not generate any apparent measurable harm and you do not stand in any obvious complicit relation to him.

When you come to know about what he is doing – the moment in which you acquire this particular piece of information in virtue of the privileged position you happen to occupy there and then – the duty of public accountability, which your colleague has forfeited, falls onto you. This is because of the interdependence of organizational roles, and in virtue of the second-personal relations of public accountability thereby established. Therefore, you ought to blow the whistle on your cunning colleague to restore the logic of public accountability that he has altered. Your action is justified as a matter of duty as an instance of the second-personal duty of public accountability he and you owe to all other members of your organization, in virtue of the role-based structural relations you all entertain within the rule-based system established with the establishment of that organization. So, to summarize:

THE PUBLIC-ACCOUNTABILITY-BASED VIEW OF WHISTLEBLOWING: A member of an organization ought to blow the whistle when she has privileged access to information concerning uses of entrusted power within her organization that contradict that power's mandate. She ought to do so in order to restore the logic of public accountability that such an alleged wrongful practice or behaviour has altered.

Notice that we are not just saying that you have a duty to report your cunning colleague's behaviour as an *entailment* of the general organizational-membership duty of public accountability. If this were our argument, we would be offering only an instrumental justification of your duty; the practice of whistleblowing would be required because it is a source of otherwise inaccessible information on organizational wrongdoing, whose disclosure is essential to re-establish disrupted relations of public accountability. This entailment is true, and it is a part of our argument; but this is not the full argument, because in this way we would fail to vindicate the practice of whistleblowing as a duty in its own right.

The crux of our argument is that, by disclosing crucial information in the first person, your action as a whistleblower *realizes in itself* the logic of public accountability that ought to govern the interactions between the members of a legitimate organization and that your cunning colleague's behaviour has altered. In the same fashion, for example, when Edward Snowden decided to meet the journalists and disclose the information on the mass-surveillance programmes of which he was aware, he made himself accountable in the first person for revealing the wrongdoing that had occurred within his organization. In this case, we can say Snowden was not merely acting in a way derivative from the organizational-membership duty of public accountability. His report is itself a specific instance of that general duty.[8]

We offer further considerations of the nature of this duty in the following chapter. For now, it bears emphasizing that characterizing the duty of whistleblowing in terms of public accountability has the distinctive feature of identifying the addressee of the report not as any designated recipient – be it an appointed officer within the organization or an external governmental agency – but rather as each and every fellow member of the organization in which the alleged wrongdoing occurs. This second-personal stance determines the moral and logical priority of relations of public accountability over other kinds of relations, in virtue of the very structure of any rule-based system.

Surely, the scope and the extent of such relations vary according to the specific nature of the organization under consideration – whether it is a public institution, a private association, a business corporation, and so on. Notably, the nature of the organization specifies the exact constituency to whom this second-personal justification is owed. In the case of public institutions, this constituency may actually be quite broad, and, for certain roles (e.g., those subject to democratic elections), it may extend to the citizenry at large.

We should also clarify that discharging the duty of whistleblowing might conflict with other duties deriving from the multiple roles each individual organizational member may have. Multiple compossible roles could generate a set of conflicting duties, such that the duty to blow the whistle is but one duty among other role-based organizational duties of membership. This condition entails that any given agent might need to balance the normative force of such different and possibly conflicting duties. The attribution of a specific weight to such duties requires a common scale that might be hard to establish on principled grounds. To get around this difficulty, a consequentialist assessment of the relative stringency of any member's duties seems a promising way forward. But is this way forward compatible with our deontological framework?

It is important to emphasize that our argument does not entail an utter disregard for any consequentialist consideration (see Ceva and Bocchiola, forthcoming). In fact, considerations of this sort should be taken into account when we discuss the practical details of how whistleblowing should be exercised in specific circumstances, in light of the impact that acting on this duty might have on an agent's capacity to fulfil other duties she might have – for example, respect for personal privacy or a professional duty of secrecy. The tension between fulfilling the duty of whistleblowing and a professional duty of secrecy (on matters concerning military operation, with an impact on both national security and individual safety) is central, for example, to the cases of Snowden and Manning we have discussed above. We revisit these points at length in the next chapter. For now, we can notice that the details of the regulation of whistleblowing should include the specific institutional arrangements that should be in place to make whistleblowing effective, as well as the concrete obligations to which this duty gives rise for specific individuals, in view of the specific role they occupy, how they came to know of the wrongdoing, and the epistemic strength of their information.

This reasoning suggests the duty of whistleblowing is not absolute, nor is the exercise of this duty unconditional. In specific circumstances, which require a case-by-case discussion, there might be weighty countervailing reasons that offer an over-arching reason not to act on the duty to blow the whistle. However, these circumstantial occurrences do not undermine our general public-accountability-based defence of the duty of whistleblowing. This duty is there, and failures to act on it may never be morally justified.

Conclusion

We have now reached an important point in our discussion of the duty of whistleblowing. We started with a critical review of the main received views in the current debate, which account, respectively, for the duty to blow the whistle on organizational wrongdoing in terms of preventing either the measurable harms thereby caused or someone's complicity in the wrongful action in question. We have scrutinized the cogency of these accounts by pinpointing their normative narrowness and epistemic demandingness.

To overcome those limitations, we have offered a novel and more comprehensive approach that grounds the duty of whistleblowing in the duty of public accountability generally binding on the members of a rule-based organization. By their interdependent status, the members of such organizations are accountable to one another for the uses they make of the power they exercise in virtue of their role. When a member, in the exercise of her organizational functions, makes use of her power according to terms that contradict those of the mandate with which that power was entrusted to her role, an inherent organizational wrong occurs. Any member of that same organization who has access to information on the alleged occurrence of such a wrongdoing has a duty to report it in order to honour – in the specific circumstances – her organizational-membership duty of public accountability.

On the basis of this summary, we can submit that our account offers a cogent normative basis for justifying the duty of whistleblowing that meets the conditions that, as we have seen in this chapter, ensue from the need to avoid the limitations of the current received harm-based and complicity-based views.

Notably, *contra* the consequentialist shortcomings of the harm-based view, we have shown that the duty of whistleblowing is grounded in the very nature of organizational membership and, therefore, is independent of the actual or expected measurable harmful consequences that the objectionable reported facts may or may not cause. In this sense, our view shares a clear deontological connotation with the complicity-based view, as well as its focus on the whistleblower's position. However, our view is more general because it grounds the duty of whistleblowing in the structural relational features of organizational membership and not in any specific and circumstantial relation in which the potential whistleblower personally stands with either the wrongdoing or the wrongdoer (notably, that of an accomplice).

While the duty to blow the whistle is a specific instance of the general organizational-membership duty of public accountability, it is a distinctive duty: it may not be entirely reduced to other ordinary professional responsibilities. This specific duty is triggered under the special circumstances in which someone acquires nonpublic information on an alleged wrongdoing within her organization. This duty applies to anyone who partakes in organizational membership in virtue of the second-personal structural relations they entertain with all the other members of a system of interdependent rule-governed roles.

This characterization implies that the justification of the duty of whistleblowing is independent of the specific tasks for which one is responsible within an organization and one's relative cognitive skills or professional expertise. Particularly, our account does not pose any demanding epistemic standard concerning the relevant information that should uphold the report.

To be sure, in keeping with the commitment to public accountability, any potential whistleblower is expected to carry the burden of proof concerning the alleged wrongdoing she reports. For this burden to be discharged, an explanation is in order of how the reported facts concern usages of entrusted power that contradict the terms of its mandate. The standard of proof of any such explanation necessarily varies in accordance with the general level of knowledge and expertise that can be reasonably presumed comes with any given role (the standard of proof that could be reasonably and generally expected of a manager or a technician is necessarily different from that which applies to a lower-level clerk or a janitor).

Unlike the other theories we have reviewed, the working of our justification of whistleblowing (which focuses on the general structural duties that pertain to organizational membership) makes our account of the standards of proof that should uphold the whistleblower's report both less demanding and more open at the same time. It is less demanding as it refers directly to the terms of the mandate with which certain powers are associated with certain roles (and not to such highly idealized tests as, e.g., that of De George's impartial observer). It is more open because it allows a generous margin of contextual adaptation to a plurality of organizational cultures and structures (either public or private) and membership levels (from the managers through to the base membership).

More should be said on what is required to make the fulfilment of this duty possible and compatible with the other (personal and organizational) duties the potential whistleblower may have. We have left this, our final task, for the next chapter.

3

Whistleblowing: Personal Trust, Secrecy, and Public Accountability

Introduction

We started our inquiry into the duty of whistleblowing by offering a conceptual analysis that revolved around the following definition of this practice:

WHISTLEBLOWING: the practice through which a member of a legitimate organization voluntarily reports some wrongdoing, allegedly occurring within that organization, with the intention that corrective action should be taken to address it.

We used the six constitutive components of this definition (action, agent, locus, object, addressee, motivation) to flesh out the distinctive features of such representative cases of whistleblowing as those of Edward Snowden and Chelsea Manning. But the definition also served as guidance for the thought experiments through which we showed the limitations of the major current justifications of the duty of whistleblowing – the harm- and the complicity-based views – and proposed our own public-accountability-based normative view of this practice. We summarized the view as follows:

THE PUBLIC-ACCOUNTABILITY-BASED VIEW OF WHISTLEBLOWING: A member of an organization ought to blow the whistle when she has privileged access to information concerning uses of entrusted power within her organization that contradict that power's mandate. She ought to do so in order to restore the logic of public accountability that such an alleged wrongful practice or behaviour has altered.

Central to this view are the characterization of the whistleblower (*any* member of an organization who happens to have privileged access to some relevant information) and the wrongdoing object of the report (a practice or behaviour whose rationale contradicts the terms of the mandate with which the power entrusted to certain rule-governed organizational roles should be exercised). The duty of whistleblowing is justified as a specific instance of the general duty of public accountability that standardly governs the second-personal relations between the members of a rule-based organization in the exercise of their functions.

This view shares many of the defining features of the other two views – notably, those concerning the voluntariness of the report; the locus where both the objectionable facts (whether unlawful or legal, but morally problematic) and their report occur (a legitimate organization); and the motivation of the report (to urge corrective action). However, our view is more general and encompassing. The duty of whistleblowing is justified even in those cases in which no measurable harm ensues from the objectionable facts, and cases that do not implicate (either directly or as an accomplice) the potential whistleblower. Moreover, our justification does not derive the duty of whistleblowing either from the ordinary specific responsibilities, or from the special cognitive skills and expertise, that any given member of an organization may have in virtue of her profession.

As argued in the previous chapter, we consider these features of our view an important advancement on the state of the current debate. Notably, our normative view of whistleblowing, in virtue of this generality, is capable of making sense of many potentially relevant forms of organizational wrongdoing and allows for a broad margin of adaptation to the details of the many nuances such a multifaceted practice may have across different organizational contexts (e.g., concerning the anonymity of the report or whether it should occur through internal or external channels). These features are all the more important as they do not come at the cost of losing either the distinctiveness of the duty to blow the whistle or its stringency.

To make this point more apparent, we devote the next section to offering some further specifications of the nature of the duty of whistleblowing that our public-accountability-based view justifies. We then move on to addressing some challenges that can be pressed against our account should the duty to blow the whistle on organizational wrongdoing come to clash with other – either personal or professional – duties the potential whistleblower may have.

The Duty of Whistleblowing: Organizational and Individual

Bluntly put, the public-accountability-based view of the duty of whistleblowing substantiates a perfect, generally binding, all-things-considered organizational duty. This duty is binding on any rule-based legitimate organization and requires, always and necessarily, establishing internal and external reporting mechanisms through which relevant organizational wrongdoings can be brought to light and, consequently, corrective action may be taken. In this sense, the duty of whistleblowing grounds primarily a *corrective organizational practice* that realizes the general organizational duty of public accountability in the specific non-ideal circumstances in which organizational wrongdoing occurs (see also Ceva and Bocchiola, forthcoming).

This duty can be discharged, as anticipated, by establishing internal as well as external reporting mechanisms. Internal mechanisms primarily address fellow members of the organization – from one's direct superior to higher levels of management – in which the objected facts have allegedly occurred. These mechanisms include safe communication channels (e.g., a hotline or a secure website for filing a report). Complex organizations might also create a designated office whose task is to collect whistleblowers' reports and, eventually, open a formal investigation, if necessary. External mechanisms, instead, are directed to such external addressees as the police or some dedicated authority responsible for providing legal advice to whistleblowers' initiatives or investigating their disclosures.[1]

These mechanisms should also include adequate protections to guarantee the safety of potential whistleblowers (notice that understanding this practice as a matter of duty rules out the provision of rewards). Anonymity could, for example, shield potential whistleblowers from the risk of retaliations (including mobbing, or even dismissal). Such a provision, however, may only be viable in large organizations, in which the whistleblower's identity might not be easy to guess. Other safeguards may provide a more substantial kind of support, including free legal assistance and, perhaps, job relocation or re-integration.

Protections of this sort are primarily meant to remove the obstacles that potential whistleblowers may encounter and that may discourage them from coming forward. In fact, the best way to see these protections, from our perspective, is to consider them as setting the conditions for the general organizational duty to translate into a specific duty to blow the whistle on organizational wrongdoing binding on individual members. When the required corrective organizational actions have been taken, and the related reporting mechanisms are in place, any member who had privileged access to information concerning a relevant kind of organizational wrongdoing (as characterized above) ought to blow the whistle by resorting to one of the established, either internal or external (as the circumstances have it), reporting channels.

It is important to note, from our perspective, that these channels identify both internal and external addressees to whom the individual duty to blow the whistle should be practically discharged. However, in virtue of its second-personal nature, this moral duty is mutually binding on the members of an organization (independently of the position they occupy in the organizational hierarchy). As argued in the previous chapter, the interdependency of organizational roles establishes those who occupy those roles as mutually accountable for the uses they make of their entrusted powers in the exercise of their rule-governed organizational functions. Therefore, each member of a rule-based organization has the second-personal moral authority to demand of her fellow members the fulfilment of the duties that come with those roles (including the duty of public accountability, of which the duty to blow the whistle is a specific instance).

This set of considerations reveals the internal complexities of the normative account of the duty of whistleblowing in our public-accountability-based view. While the duty to establish whistleblowing as an organizational corrective practice is perfect and generally binding at the organizational level, the specific duty to blow the whistle on any given instance of organizational wrongdoing is imperfect and conditional for any one member of the organization. This means that, should the organizational duty not be discharged, no individual action is necessarily required as a moral 'ought', while it may still be permissible and laudable.

This line of reasoning makes normative sense of the intuitive evaluation we have given of Snowden's and Manning's disclosures as belonging to the domain of the supererogatory. Neither of their reports could be required as a matter of duty, because neither of their organizations had established the corrective reporting practices that their general duty of public accountability in fact required (as the ordeals the two whistleblowers had to endure unmistakably illustrate). Absent these conditions, in our view, Snowden's and Manning's decisions to leak the information to which they had privileged access on wrongdoings that had occurred within their organizations was arguably good and permissible, but not required.

A general implication of this argument is that, when the required organizational reporting procedures have been established, rather than reaching out to the media, potential whistleblowers ought to file their reports following the (either internal or external) channels these procedures provide for. In this sense, the duty of whistleblowing does not justify unauthorized tips and leaks (Sagar, 2013, ch. 6; Boot 2017, 2018). However, unauthorized tips and leaks may still be permissible insofar as they are the only way of bringing organizational wrongdoing to light.

This reasoning makes these forms of unauthorized whistleblowing an *extrema ratio* that applies when internal and external authorized reporting mechanisms are either missing or, arguably, have been exhausted and proved ineffective. We think this is a further important advancement our public-accountability-based view makes on the state of the debate. Namely, it allows distinguishing permissible from required whistleblowing, as a matter both of organizational practice (always required) and of individual behaviour (conditionally required).

This distinction is important, we believe, because it clarifies the normative characterization of the distinctive public function whistleblowing may have within a general theory of public ethics. The qualification of the stringency of the organizational and individual duties at stake also allows us to address the worry that the fulfilment of the duty to blow the whistle may be over-demanding for any individual member of the organization in which a relevant wrongdoing allegedly occurs.

While our discussion so far has led to these two significant results, our case for the duty of whistleblowing as a corrective organizational practice may not yet be put to rest. A couple of further concerns could be raised to challenge the plausibility of this duty.

As illustrated with reference to the debates surrounding the cases of Snowden and Manning, whistleblowers have been often looked at suspiciously from various sides – including the organizational management, their co-workers, and the general public – because, *inter alia*, of the potential risks this practice implies for the quality of interpersonal relations. According to this commonly understood sense, whistleblowing has the supposed unpalatable consequence of generating a climate of mutual suspicion and distrust within an organization. Crudely put, the allegation is that whistleblowing undermines interpersonal relations by creating a Big Brother kind of environment in which personal trust and group loyalty are supplanted by mutual diffidence and the anxiety that may derive from the feeling of being constantly under scrutiny. This wariness is heightened in the case of external whistleblowing because it may lead to weakening of public trust in an organization by diminishing its credibility.

In the remainder of this chapter, we would like to rescue our normative public-accountability-based view of whistleblowing from these common critiques. In particular, we attend in more or less explicit terms to two main worries that underlie these critiques. These worries can be couched in terms of the fear that discharging the duty to blow the whistle on organizational wrongdoing may clash, first, with the personal duties of confidentiality that may ensue from relations of personal trust, as well as, second, those of secrecy that may apply to some professional roles. We discuss each of these two worries in turn in the following two sections (see, also and extensively, Ceva and Bocchiola, forthcoming).

Whistleblowing and the Violation of Personal Trust

Consider the following scenario:

Anna is a public officer in charge of making a job appointment. Bruce is a candidate for that job.

Bruce owes money to Anna because of some previous personal agreement between the two of them. In the effort to recover the loan, Anna wishes to appoint Bruce on the agreement that Bruce will use a part of his salary each month to pay back his debt to Anna. Bruce is qualified for the job, and luck has it that no other candidate applies for this position. So, eventually, Anna hires Bruce.

This is a scenario of political corruption (Ceva and Ferretti, 2017; Ceva and Bocchiola, forthcoming) that fits our characterization of organizational wrongdoing. Recall that this characterization points at an alteration of the order of public rules because of a use of entrusted power in contradiction with the terms of the mandate with which that power was assigned to a certain organizational role and, therefore, in keeping with which it should be exercised.

As detailed in the previous chapter, organizations are structures of interdependent rule-governed embodied roles to which specific powers are assigned to perform specific functions in keeping with a generally known mandate. Such a structure generates a system of rights and duties that people hold in virtue of their organizational membership.

Political corruption occurs when those who

occupy such roles within public institutions (the officeholders) use the power associated with their role for the pursuit of an agenda whose rationale may not be publicly vindicated in accordance with the mandate for which the power associated with a specific office should be exercised (Ceva, 2018; Ceva and Ferretti, 2017).[2]

In this light, Anna's behaviour is problematic, as an instance of political corruption. Even if the appointment of Bruce does not apparently break any law (recall that Bruce is qualified for the job) and does not have an obvious negative impact on the employment opportunities of others (Bruce happens to be the only candidate for the job), Anna's behaviour is nonetheless wrong *qua* corrupt, because it consists in a publicly unaccountable use of her entrusted power of appointment.

Notice that Anna's behaviour is not only personally problematic. Because Anna acts on the power of appointment that belongs to her organizational role, the use she makes of this power in the exercise of her functions qualifies as an instance of organizational wrongdoing (see Ceva and Ferretti, 2018). In other words, Anna does not act in her personal capacity, but in her capacity as the member of an organization. In this specific capacity, Anna hires Bruce with the intent to recover the money Bruce owes her; but recovery of a personal credit is surely not an item for an agenda whose rationale can withstand public scrutiny as a reason for her action coherent with the terms of the mandate with which the power of appointment was presumably given to Anna, in her capacity as the holder of a public office. Therefore, Anna's action is an organizational wrong, in our sense, as an instance of political corruption.

Now, imagine a possible development of this scenario:

After the selection, Anna goes to lunch with Charles, a friendly co-worker. While they enjoy their meal together, Anna tells Charles how lucky she was she could appoint Bruce without any trouble so she can finally have her money back. This way, Charles comes to know of a possible wrongdoing Anna committed in the exercise of her function within the organization both Anna and Charles work for. The relation is complicated by the fact that Charles apprehends this information about the behaviour of his co-worker in virtue of the personal relation in which he stands to Anna. This specific circumstance makes it extremely unlikely that anyone else will ever come to know of the surreptitious agreement between Anna and Bruce, unless Charles speaks up.

What ought Charles, morally speaking, to do? Ought Charles, necessarily, to blow the whistle on Anna? Or ought Charles to keep Anna's secret for himself?

Whistleblowing implies reporting on somebody – from a mere acquaintance, to a friend, to maybe even a relative – whom the whistleblower knows within the organization in which the two work. A potential whistleblower (such as Charles) is therefore caught between the duties deriving from the personal relationship she entertains with the person who is the object of the potential revelation and the duties of organizational membership (including the duty to blow the whistle on organizational wrongdoing) that, as already seen, are independent of her personal ties.

A common way to frame this issue consists in presenting it as a conflict of someone's duties of *privacy* and *transparency* (see Ceva and Bocchiola, forthcoming).

In broad strokes, privacy is the capacity of an individual to enjoy a condition in which she is free from constant direct or indirect observation, being in control over the access others have to the information that concerns her.[3] A commitment to privacy entails that certain personal information ought to remain confidential (absent overriding reasons – see Solove, 2008, 2011). This commitment is important, *inter alia*, to cement valuable interpersonal relations. Most of these relations, such as those of friendship, involve confidential exchanges of pieces of personal information that come with an expectation that they remain between the parties involved (so that the control over the access to a piece of information is preserved). If we value privacy so understood, the duty of whistleblowing may be questioned as a violation of the duty of confidentiality, a violation that has the negative consequence of fostering mutual distrust between the members of an organization.[4]

Transparency, on the other hand, consists in the idea that some information – which is likely to affect people's everyday life – should not be concealed (see Hood and Heald, 2006). Advocates of transparency claim that, vis-à-vis certain kinds of information and in certain circumstances, people should be in the condition of acquiring any such information and not just the facts that others are independently willing to provide. This argument has often been made in relation to matters of public concern that include, we can safely say, the way entrusted power is exercised by those who hold public office. If transparency, so understood, is a value, whistleblowing (as an instrument for enhancing transparency) is morally permissible and, in fact, often required.

Privacy and transparency are central values in interpersonal relations because they inform people's expectations concerning the access to important information. However, the joint realization of these two values (and the fulfilment of the duties they justify) is problematic. This problem is apparent to the extent that the revelation of some information for the sake of transparency implies a violation of someone else's privacy. For example, realizing organizational transparency could imply asking some of the members to waive control over some personal information or asking others to commit a breach of their personal duty of confidentiality. Scenarios of this sort are typical in cases of whistleblowing, whose justification may be seen to depend significantly on the relative weight of the two values.

In our example, if Charles did not report on Anna on the grounds of privacy, Charles would honour the confidentiality that characterizes their friendly relation, but Anna's misbehaviour would remain unnoticed, thus hampering the transparency of their organization in a straightforward sense. But if Charles decided to honour transparency, his revelations would violate the relation of privacy – and the related expectation of confidentiality – upon which Anna was acting when she revealed to Charles the agreement that led to Bruce's appointment. In either case, whether Charles blows the whistle on Anna or not, it seems Charles is doomed to frustrate an important value and sacrifice some morally relevant normative commitment.

Therefore, it seems the only way forward for Charles is to trade off the value of privacy against that of transparency. Given the importance of the values at stake, Charles cannot simply flip a coin; a principled solution is in order to guide Charles's action. For this solution to be in sight, a generally valid exchange rate between privacy and transparency must be established.

A possible way to fix this exchange rate is by looking at the harm Anna's behaviour could cause to the organization for which both Anna and Charles work or, more extensively, some dimension of the public interest (see Kumar and Santoro, 2017). The evaluation of this harm should then be balanced against the consequences of the loss of Anna's privacy were Charles to decide to blow the whistle on her. On this ground, Charles's whistleblowing seems unjustified because Anna's behaviour caused no measurable harm (no other candidates showed up) and she did not break any law (Bruce was qualified for the job). On this consequentialist reading, transparency may be sacrificed in the name of privacy and, therefore, Charles is not justified in blowing the whistle on Anna.

Following our criticism of the harm-based view of whistleblowing in the previous chapter, we think this conclusion is problematic on two grounds. First, to say Charles is not justified in blowing the whistle on Anna means letting Anna off the hook; recall that Charles comes to know of Anna and Bruce's agreement only because Anna tells this to Charles in confidence, and, therefore, we have no basis to think the agenda underpinning Anna's decision to hire Bruce could become known otherwise. The conclusion above is problematic because, as anticipated, there is at least one sense in which Anna's action is inherently wrong, independently of its consequences: it is an instance of organizational wrongdoing that goes under the name of political corruption. Anna's behaviour is wrong in the sense of being corrupt because it consists in her using the power of appointment that comes with her organizational role for the pursuit of an agenda (the recovery of Bruce's debt to her) that cannot be publicly indicated. In this light, and in the circumstances, Anna's behaviour should not be so easily tolerated, even when no measurable harm (to the public interest or otherwise) follows.

The second problem of this consequentialist way

out of the privacy-vs-transparency dilemma concerns the kind of solution it wishes to provide. This solution aspires to offer a third-personal, objective measure of the harm caused by and to the agents involved. However, in the case under scrutiny – and, in fact, in many other relevant ones – identifying such a measure is a chimeric undertaking, because it involves many dimensions (material and immaterial) that may be quite diffused and difficult to quantify and weigh against each other. Surely, these reservations apply to the case of public interest, whose definition is distinctively blurred.[5]

Notably, the kinds of harm implicated in cases of whistleblowing are neither specific nor determined. At the very least, the justification of Charles's course of action is exposed to the erratic consideration of the context and nature of the harm caused by Anna's behaviour. Moreover, the exact nature of the relation between Anna and Charles (whether they are, for example, mere acquaintances, life-long friends, or perhaps siblings) matters too for assessing the strength of their reciprocal personal duties, and, consequently, for appreciating the kind of damage a possible breach of Anna's privacy would cause to their bond of trust in the specific circumstances.

In light of these two problems, we suggest that to

adopt this consequentialist approach to justifying whistleblowing would, at best, lead to a merely circumstantial outcome and, therefore, fail to provide a principled solution that could deliver normatively cogent guidance for action. Specifically, to look at the justification of whistleblowing from the perspective of the values of privacy and transparency seems to provide the potential whistleblower with two sets of morally relevant considerations that pull him in different directions, but without any normatively cogent guidance to choose between them. From this perspective, whistleblowing could at most be seen as a conscientious *extrema ratio*, a decision one is justified to make only as the outcome of a tragic choice vis-à-vis some grave wrongdoing whose magnitude would be too large to ignore.

We think the public-accountability-based view we have proposed in this book can fruitfully offer a fresh and normatively cogent perspective on this scenario. In particular, we suggest that looking at this scenario from our proposed perspective allows us to grasp the complexities of the relations involved in it. To see these complexities, we should focus on the distinction between the two different capacities in which the protagonists of the scenario interact – that is, as fellow members of an organization and as parties to a friendly relation. The former is a public kind of relation because it is governed by rules that are public in the sense of being generally known. The latter is typically personal. In virtue of this characterization, the former should respond to a logic of public accountability, the latter to one of personal trust.

It is critical to note that the distinction between personal trust and public accountability falls orthogonally on that between privacy and transparency, and provides a second-personal approach to justifying whistleblowing. Let us refer back to our illustrative scenario to lay out this justification.

Anna entertains a personal, friendly relation with Charles. This relation is characterized by personal trust in a certain degree of confidentiality concerning the information Anna and Charles exchange. But, we want to suggest, this personal kind of relation between Anna and Charles – and the bonds of personal trust it entails – are beside the point. Insofar as Anna has acted in her capacity of an officeholder and has hired Bruce in virtue of the power she has acquired because of her role, she is directly accountable to Charles – and, in fact, any other co-worker – for the uses she has made of her power. And the justification Anna owes for her exercise of power must show the coherence of the rationale of the agenda that informs this exercise with the terms of the mandate with which that power was entrusted to her in virtue of her organizational membership. So, Anna cannot really appeal to the value of privacy and hold Charles to a duty of confidentiality when she reveals her surreptitious agreement with Bruce. She has acted in her capacity of an officeholder, and, as we have already argued, she has a second-personal duty to account publicly for the uses she has made of her power.

Unfortunately, in the circumstances, Anna cannot possibly justify her behaviour in this way. Her decision to hire Bruce responds to an agenda whose rationale has nothing to do with the terms of the mandate with which the power of appointment was entrusted to her. As argued in chapter 2, this condition shifts the duty of public accountability onto Charles. In these non-ideal circumstances, Charles's duty to blow the whistle on Anna is justified in order to restore the logic of public accountability Anna's misbehaviour has altered.

Remarkably, Charles's disclosure is not justified in response to a generic third-personal duty of transparency he may owe to the organization for which he (as well as Anna) works. Charles's disclosure is justified as a specific instance of the general second-personal duty of public accountability he owes to all other members of their organization in virtue of the role-based relations they entertain. These relations are logically and morally prior to other kinds of relations in virtue of the very structure of an organization as an interdependent system of rule-governed roles.

We can certainly continue to think the privacy-driven critique of whistleblowing has been sound in underscoring that this practice is likely to undermine bonds of trust at the personal level (Anna and Charles's friendship might be challenged by Charles's blowing the whistle). However, this is not a sufficient reason to lose our faith in the general merits of whistleblowing as a corrective organizational practice to restore the relations of public accountability that such forms of organizational wrongdoing as political corruption may disrupt.

In this sense, our justification of the duty of whistleblowing is a contribution in the domain of *public* ethics.

Whistleblowing and the Violation of Secrecy

We have built our normative view of the duty of whistleblowing on the claim that the members of rule-based legitimate organizations owe to each other a duty of public accountability. On this basis, we have developed a relational justification of the organizational corrective practice of whistleblowing as a matter of duty.

One implication of our view is that external (and not only internal) whistleblowing is a matter of duty, thus including both ordinary cases in which a member of an organization addresses her complaints to her supervisor and cases in which, failing internal channels, the potential whistleblower goes outside the organization. Therefore, we can see that both Snowden (internal and, subsequently, external channels) and Manning (external channels) acted on this duty.

We opened our argument in this chapter by fleshing out the two dimensions of the duty of whistleblowing: as a matter of organizational practices and of individual behaviour. As explained, at the organizational level, this duty is perfect and generally binding. Its content consists in the establishment of safe reporting mechanisms (e.g., reporting authorities and measures against retaliation). Once this organizational duty has been discharged, individuals facing relevant organizational wrongdoing have a duty to blow the whistle through these mechanisms. This individual duty, we have submitted, is imperfect and conditional.

This implication might raise the concern that

honouring these two demands of public accountability (which substantiate the duty of whistleblowing) might undermine important policies to the extent that their realization requires secrecy (see Thompson, 1999). This may apply, in a straightforward sense, to matters of public security (e.g., surveillance systems) as well as to such political negotiations as those concerning particularly sensitive issues (e.g., the regulation of abortion), negotiations which may require a great deal of background work behind closed doors in order not to upset public opinion.

Are organizational practices and individual actions of whistleblowing morally required in any such circumstance? To elaborate, does our public-accountability-based normative view of whistleblowing also justify a duty to report relevant forms of organizational wrongdoing that involve information protected by professional duties of secrecy (e.g., work contracts that include a confidentiality clause)? Or, alternatively, should we consider whistleblowing in these circumstances as a supererogatory matter of individual conscience that may be carried out only through unauthorized actions (e.g., leaks to the media as a form of civil disobedience)? [6]

Our response to this challenge derives directly from our normative account of organizational roles centred on the idea of public accountability (see also Ceva and Bocchiola, forthcoming). If our claim concerning the centrality of the commitment to public accountability in any rule-based legitimate organization is sound, important implications follow for the establishment of secrecy-motivated constraints on the performance of those roles. Notably, while there might be contingent reasons of *prudence* that speak in favour of such constraints (as, e.g., in the vexed case of matters of national security that emerged, for instance, in the cases of Snowden's as well as Manning's disclosures), the very nature of these organizations dictates the *moral* priority of the requirements of public accountability.

When we make this claim, we are not recasting the privacy-vs-transparency dilemma in a different guise; to appeal to the general second-personal membership duty of public accountability is not the same as falling back on the third-personal organizational duty of transparency. Notably, unlike the case of transparency, to discharge the duty of public accountability does not require, nor does it entail, full accessibility and the systematic denial of secrecy.[7] Public accountability is, rather, a moral regulative idea that ought to guide the action of those who occupy organizational roles within a rule-based organization.

As explained, in virtue of their institutional membership, officeholders ought to act in such a way that makes it possible for their action's rationale to withstand public scrutiny. This means that they must be in the position of demonstrating the coherence of the rationale of their action with the terms of the mandate with which their entrusted power should be exercised. So, although certain uses of their power of office may be covered by secrecy (and, therefore, are not fully accessible as transparency demands), any such use should always be publicly justifiable in accordance with the terms of the mandate with which that power was associated with their specific organizational role. To put it in other words, even in those cases in which duties of secrecy are justified with respect to a certain office, this does not absolve the officeholder of the general duty to act in such a way that the rationale of her action *could* be publicly justified (even if the case of her having to provide such a justification is an eventuality that might never actually materialize). In this sense, to honour this duty is a matter of public ethics.

The corrective practice of whistleblowing (in both its institutional and individual manifestations, as detailed above) is a specific instantiation of this general structural duty of public accountability in non-ideal circumstances vis-à-vis relevant organizational wrongdoing. Therefore, in answer to the challenge, we concur with a growing consensus in the debate that whistleblowing is also justified in those cases that include revelations concerning relevant forms of organizational wrongdoing that involve information covered by secrecy. But, unlike many of these views, we reject the implication that, in these cases, whistleblowing takes the form of an individual conscientious action akin to civil disobedience.

Rather, we argue, safe internal and external reporting mechanisms should include provisions that cover these cases too. So, while Snowden's and Manning's unauthorized disclosures may be excused, given the non-ideal circumstances in which they had to operate, well-functioning organizations do not tolerate such individual conscientious (and potentially unlawful) acts of leaking as those performed by our epitomic whistleblowers. Well-functioning organizations establish internal and external reporting channels through which individual members may honour their mutual duties of public accountability in non-ideal circumstances.

The working details of such channels (e.g., ombudsmen, special committees, governmental agencies) depend by and large on specific legal arrangements and policies that exceed the boundaries and competences of philosophical theorizing. We would like to stress a different aspect instead. Our argument shows that the attention of many current discussions of whistleblowing (in philosophy and also in the political and legal debate) as a form of conscientious individual unlawful action of dissent only captures a small and residual portion of what whistleblowing is about.

The most important conclusion of our argument in this chapter is that whistleblowing is an essential component of any good organizational practice to counteract such important forms of organizational wrongdoing as political corruption.

Conclusion

In this chapter, we have clarified the twofold nature – organizational and individual – of the duty of whistleblowing in accordance with our public-accountability-based normative view of this practice. We have also corroborated our defence of this view by addressing two main challenges that can be raised against its plausibility and stringency.

The first challenge concerns the alleged conflict

between the membership duty to blow the whistle on organizational wrongdoing and the personal duties of confidentiality that characterize personal relations of mutual trust. We have responded to this challenge by arguing that it rests, in fact, on a failure to grasp the specificities of two dimensions of the interpersonal relations that whistleblowing involves: a public and a personal one.

One might well say that, by making certain personal information publicly available for the sake of transparency, whistleblowing violates the privacy of those who are the object of the revelation. This violation is in fact problematic to the extent that it implies a breach of confidentiality, and because it might have the consequence of undermining personal bonds of trust between the members of the same organization.

However, while individual acts of whistleblowing might have this consequence when they occur in isolation, the practice of whistleblowing per se need not be vulnerable to the same critique. In fact, we have shown that, appropriately qualified and regulated, the practice of whistleblowing has the capacity of enhancing, in non-ideal conditions, the quality of the relations of public accountability between the members of a rule-based organization, and, therefore, the general trust within such an organization and between those who hold office within it.

We have then addressed a second and final challenge concerning whether whistleblowing is justified as a matter of duty even in those cases in which professional duties of secrecy hold. From the vantage point of our public-accountability-based view, we have argued that the corrective organizational practice of whistleblowing is justified as a duty even in these circumstances. The fulfilment of this duty at both the organizational and individual levels requires the establishment of safe internal and external reporting mechanisms irreducible to the development of legal protections for those who decide to break the law and go public with unauthorized revelations.

On this basis, we have suggested that the common view of whistleblowing as an individual conscientious *extrema ratio* against organizational wrongdoing is only the tip of the iceberg. Understandably, it has attracted a great deal of scholarly and public attention in view of its urgency and damaging consequences in the lives of many courageous individuals. However, a full normative discussion of whistleblowing should go deeper and offer a more systematic and less emergency-driven analysis of the issue.

Our intent in this book has been to present a conceptually articulated and normatively grounded account of the duty of whistleblowing that goes exactly in that direction.

Conclusion

This book has revolved around the question of whether the practice of whistleblowing may be justified as a matter of moral duty.

In the current public and philosophical debates, whistleblowing has frequently been presented as a morally troublesome practice to the extent that it involves the breaking of promissory obligations and general duties of organizational loyalty and confidentiality. What is more, many concrete instances of this practice have entailed high personal costs for the whistleblowers, as well as social costs in the form of damage to the public reputation of the organizations and people who are the objects of the whistleblowers' disclosures. As a consequence, the justification of a duty of whistleblowing as a practice has lost plausibility, while individual decisions to blow the whistle have been generally confined to the domain of supererogatory acts. The exemplary vicissitudes of Edward Snowden and Chelsea Manning unmistakably illustrate these dynamics.

Even those commentators who are the most inclined to see the virtues of this practice have tended to regard whistleblowing as a last resort confined to situations of extreme danger to people or the environment. What is more, the justification of whistleblowing as a matter of duty has had quite a restrictive interpretation. Some have argued, for example, that whistleblowing is morally required only when there is epistemically solid evidence of the occurrence of some serious organizational wrongdoing, and blowing the whistle is necessary either to prevent or stop a measurable harm or to avoid someone's complicity with that wrongdoing, at a reasonable cost for the whistleblower. In any other circumstance, whistleblowing could be permissible and perhaps even laudable, but certainly not required as a moral 'ought'.

In this book, we have presented and defended a different normative view of the duty of whistleblowing as an organizational corrective practice: the public-accountability-based view. According to this view, the duty of whistleblowing is justified when there is a member of an organization who has privileged access to information concerning uses of entrusted power within her organization that contradict that power's mandate. She ought to blow the whistle in order to restore the logic of public accountability that the alleged occurrence of that wrongful practice or behaviour has altered.

The normative strength of this duty is a matter of second-personal authority, in the sense that it is owed to any one member of a rule-based organization by any other, in virtue of the interdependence of the organizational roles they occupy. It is in this exact sense that the normative strength of this duty does not derive from legal norms and sanctions (binding in the third person), but from the constitutive (second-personal) features of organizational structures.

The practice of whistleblowing is thus justified as a matter of duty because, in a first sense, it is a source of information on organizational wrongdoing, information that would be otherwise inaccessible. What is more, whistleblowing is also justified in a second non-instrumental sense because it instantiates the general organizational duty of public accountability in non-ideal circumstances.

Our normative account of the instantiation of this general duty in the practice of whistleblowing is internally complex. While the duty to establish whistleblowing as an organizational corrective practice is perfect and generally binding at the organizational level, the specific duty to blow the whistle on any given instance of organizational wrongdoing is imperfect and conditional for any individual member of the organization. Should the organizational duty not be discharged, no individual action is necessarily required as a moral 'ought', while it may still be permissible and laudable. This is a lesson we can learn from Snowden's and Manning's stories. The organizational wrongdoings they had witnessed, and their status of membership within the organizations in which such wrongdoings had allegedly occurred, make a strong case for justifying their actions as instances of the organizational duty of public accountability. On the view we have defended, that duty ought to have been discharged by their respective organizations first, by establishing safe internal and external reporting mechanisms. Failing such mechanisms, laudable actions of extraordinary individuals seem to be everything that is left.

We think our public-accountability-based view of the duty of whistleblowing has the merit of being quite comprehensive, but distinctive. It is distinctive because it identifies a duty that is not limited, or reducible, to other either personal or professional responsibilities individuals ordinarily have.

It is comprehensive because it covers many significantly objectionable organizational practices and individual behaviours that are inherently morally problematic (as instances of organizational wrongdoing), even if they are not unlawful and do not apparently cause any measurable harm. Whistleblowing retains its nature as a duty independently of any implication of the whistleblower either in executing the objectionable behaviour or in setting up the objectionable organizational practice. Any member of a rule-based organization may find herself in the position of being a whistleblower, regardless of her cognitive skills or professional expertise in appreciating, gathering, and processing the relevant information to uphold the report.

The term 'whistleblowing' first appeared in the public debate as a metaphor to describe those professionals who were disclosing privileged information about the safety of a product. Therefore, 'whistleblowing' has occupied a prominent role in many discussions of professional ethics. In this book, we have made a case to show that political theorists too should concern themselves with the discussion of this practice as a matter of public ethics, which characterizes the structural responses that ought to be given to such instances of organizational wrongdoing as political corruption.

Conclusion

In this sense, our general aim in this book has been to show how 'whistleblowing' is not merely a rhetorically catchy term alluding to any sort of disclosure concerning organizational wrongdoing. Rather, it identifies a specific category in the realm of practical normativity.

Notes

Introduction

1 The actual origin of the term 'whistleblowing' (or 'whistle-blowing') is unknown. Its use might be traced back, as far as we know, to the nineteenth century, and somehow became part of common parlance in the English-speaking world. For example, in 1934, the English writer P. G. Wodehouse used the term in *Right Ho, Jeeves* (2010, p. 306). Similarly, the American novelist Raymond Chandler used this expression in *The Long Goodbye* (1953, p. 70).

1 Defining Whistleblowing

1 Vandekerckhove (2006, ch. 1) reviews the usages of the term 'whistleblowing' from a historical perspective.

2 According to Davis (2003, p. 539), 'whistleblowing is not so much of a settled practice as a

growing collection of acts in search of a unifying analysis'.

3 For a comprehensive view of the state of the art across different disciplines, see Brown et al. (2014).

4 Other authors, such as, for example, Near and Miceli (1985) and Chambers (1995), stress the role of public interest in the underlying motivations for blowing the whistle.

5 Jubb (1999) argues for the need for a restricted definition of whistleblowing.

6 'Spy', 'informer', and 'rat' are among the derogatory names whistleblowers have been called. See, for instance, the stories collected in Westin (1981) and Glazer and Glazer (1989).

7 This definition encompasses the shared aspects included in many standard accounts of whistleblowing. See, for example, Lewis et al. (2014, p. 4) and Near and Miceli (1985, p. 4).

8 We say 'typically' because, when reporting certain wrongdoings is mandatory, failure to report implies personal liability. When someone files a report in these circumstances, we may say that a threat of sorts occurs (see Tsahuridu and Vandekerckhove, 2008). But this is a matter of contingent legal arrangement that does not per se invalidate the standard characterization of whistleblowing.

9 Delmas (2015), for example, discusses unauthorized disclosures in relation to government whistleblowing. Sagar (2013, ch. 6) offers a critical perspective on this issue.

10 One may think that this characteristic is incoherent with the original metaphor that sees the whistle-blower as the referee in a game. The reason is that the referee could be viewed as 'external' because he is not one of the players. While we do not think we should make this unreflected metaphor determine our philosophical thinking, we can also say that the referee is not an external authority to whom the players should report but has a codified constitutive role *within* the game.

11 On the private/public dimension of organizations, see, e.g., Bovens (1998, ch. 2).

12 Bell ringing is similar to what Feinberg (1990, p. 245) calls a 'civic duty to report criminals', which is a duty 'presupposed by our legal system and implicitly recognized by it in many ways'.

13 Standards of evidence are central to De George's (2010, p. 312) and Davis's (1996, p. 11) accounts of justified whistleblowing. Because these works offer normative assessments, rather than pure descriptions, of whistleblowing, we shall revisit them in the next chapter.

14 In the current debate, the addressee is usually referred to as the 'recipient'. The choice of the term 'addressee' is coherent with the general approach of the book: focusing on the action of whistleblowing (and, hence, the agent) to see whether it can have the status of a duty. What is crucial is, therefore, to whom the agent *addresses* the report, rather than what another agent does or is expected to do when she receives it (which is a consequence, not a consti-

tutive element, of whistleblowing – we shall touch upon this issue in passing).

15 The distinction between internal and external whistleblowing is standard in the debate. See De George (2010) and Davis (2003).

16 This provision is part of the US legislation on whistleblowing. According to the 2010 Dodd–Frank Wall Street Reform and Consumer Protection Act, whistleblowers who provide information to the Securities and Exchange Commission about a company's violation of some securities law are entitled to a reward.

17 Glenn Greenwald (2013) published the first article on Snowden's revelations on 5 June 2013. Since then, the resonance of Snowden's case can hardly be overestimated as it has also been the subject of a major film (*Snowden*) directed by Oliver Stone in 2016.

18 Among the many classified documents Manning leaked, the most influential have been the so-called Afghan War Diary (WikiLeaks, 2010a) and the Iraq War Logs (WikiLeaks, 2010b).

19 On the Granai events, see Gall and Shah (2009). On the detainees' conditions at Guantánamo, see Leigh et al. (2011).

20 On 28 November 2010, a group of newspapers – *El País*, *Der Spiegel*, *Le Monde*, the *Guardian*, and the *New York Times* – agreed to publish 220 'diplomatic cables' – i.e., classified documents containing analyses and evaluations of different countries and their leaders prepared by US diplomats around the word and directed to the US State Department.

These cables, dating between 28 December 1966 and 28 February 2010, were disclosed by WikiLeaks (2010c). For a commentary on Manning's report in Cablegate, see Meyers (2010).

21 Erin Brockovich tells her story in Brockovich (2001). This case became quite famous thanks to Steven Soderbergh's movie *Erin Brockovich*.

22 Of course, a journalist who reported an organizational wrongdoing occurring within her media organization could be considered a whistleblower (if the other elements are present).

23 There is a general tendency in the media to assign the label 'whistleblower' to anybody who induces a public accusation. A recent example concerns the 2017 sex scandals in the movie industry, in which a number of celebrities decided to speak out in order to bring to an end the abuses perpetrated by actors, directors, and producers against actresses and actors, especially at the early stages of their careers. Public accusations might be a form of whistleblowing, but not necessarily. The key features we have illustrated in this chapter intend to isolate a specific referent for cases of whistleblowing as an organizational reporting practice. This is not to say that other forms of reporting wrongdoing are less valuable or interesting. But having a clear account of what whistleblowing characteristically is helps to distinguish and name different form of reports while we try to stand clear of risks of polysemy and conceptual mix-ups.

2 *The Practice of Whistleblowing as a Duty*

1 This is sometimes the case when whistleblowing is presented as an instance of civil disobedience (for a discussion of the claim, see, for example, Brownlee (2016); Delmas (2015); Scheuerman (2014)).

2 Lepora and Goodin (2013) offer a clear overview of the complexities of the idea of complicity. While we refer to their analysis, we do not necessarily endorse their conclusions, whose assessment falls outside the boundaries of this book.

3 Obviously, there could be cases in which people whose skills and competences do not match up with those of, say, Snowden or Manning have fortuitous access to some relevant information. And it is true that, sometimes, a whistleblower is just somebody who happens to be at the right place, at the right time. A sound and cogent theory of the duty of whistleblowing should be able to include these instances, while it must remain the case that a lucky hunch is not enough for a principled defence of the duty of whistleblowing.

4 This is a further sense in which, as anticipated, resort to the metaphor of the whistleblower as the referee of a game is suggestive but conceptually inaccurate. It is the very role of the referee to blow the whistle on a foul. Therefore, she is under a professional obligation to act.

5 Seumas Miller (2017, p. 210) makes a similar point concerning the redundancy of the category of 'internal whistleblowing' with respect to the

good reporting practices that any 'ethically healthy' organization standardly has (or should have). Our critical considerations here extend also to external whistleblowing – e.g., when a professional ought to report some organizational malpractice to the police or some other judicial authority.

6 This is a familiar point in the contemporary debate on the 'good Samaritan': namely, 'a stranger who is not particularly qualified, professionally, to help, and who happens to be at the critical place, at the critical time' (Fabre, 2002, p. 129). Whether good Samaritanism generates a duty of assistance is a complex issue that goes beyond the scope of our inquiry. For an overview, see Seglow (2004) and Singer (1972, 2009). Davis (1996, p. 7) suggests that a whistleblower is a 'minimally decent Samaritan'.

7 This idea of accountability entails what Hart has called 'role-responsibility', the idea that 'whenever a person occupies a distinctive place or office in a social organization, to which specific duties are attached to provide for the welfare of others or to advance in some specific way the aims or purposes of the organization, he is properly said to be responsible for the performance of these duties, or for doing what is necessary to fulfil them' (Hart, 2008, p. 212). For a broader discussion of how normative ideals apply to the evaluation of the inherent normative properties of structured forms of human interactions, see Ceva (2016).

8 This means, to put it in a somewhat more formal fashion, that the general organizational-membership

duty of public accountability and the specific duty to blow the whistle on organizational wrongdoing stand in a contributive rather than in a merely causal relation (see Raz, 1986, p. 178).

3 Whistleblowing:
Personal Trust, Secrecy, and Public Accountability

1 The former kind of authority was created by the House for Whistleblowers Act (Wet Huis voor klokkenluiders), which came into effect in the Netherlands on 1 July 2016. The latter kind of authority is present in a number of national regulations of whistleblowing including the recent Italian law that has entrusted this responsibility to the National Anti-Corruption Authority (ANAC).

2 Notice that this characterization implies that corruption may or may not entail illegal action.

3 We only have the space here for embracing this largely accepted view of privacy because it captures the aspects of this idea that are particularly relevant for our discussion. For an overview of the philosophical debate on privacy, see, for example, DeCew (1997), Inness (1992), Moore (2010), and Solove (2008).

4 See Rachels (1975). On the relevance of privacy for political relationships and public justification, see Mokrosińska (2017).

5 We do not have the space to account for the many controversies and the sources of vagueness concerning references to the public interest. We trust that the

reader will be roughly familiar with various attempts to address these issues (see, to name but some classic works, Flathman, 1966; Held, 1970; King et al. 2010), and hope to give sufficiently strong arguments to show that a different but more stringent deontological justification of whistleblowing is available.

6 For a discussion, see Sagar (2013), chs. 5 and 6. Whistleblowing is discussed as a form of civil disobedience in Bok (1980), Delmas (2015), and Jubb (1999).

7 In this respect, O'Neill (2006, p. 77) has argued that mere transparency might not be enough to counteract a misplaced use of secrecy, because it could produce 'a flow of information ... analogous to a flow of water' that does not take 'account of the audiences it is meant to benefit, or of the epistemic and ethical norms that are indispensable for adequate communication'.

References

Bok, S. (1980). Whistleblowing and Professional Responsibility. *New York University Education Quarterly*, 11(4), pp. 2–10

Boot, E. R. (2017). Classified Public Whistleblowing: How to Justify a Pro Tanto Wrong. *Social Theory and Practice*, 43(3), pp. 541–67

Boot, E. R. (2018). No Right to Classified Public Whistleblowing. *Ratio Juris*, forthcoming.

Bovens, M. (1998). *The Quest for Responsibility: Accountability and Citizenship in Complex Organizations*. Cambridge University Press

Bowie, N. (1982). *Business Ethics*. Englewood Cliffs, NJ: Prentice Hall

Brockovich, E. (2001). *Take It from Me: Life's a Struggle but You Can Win*. New York: McGraw-Hill

Brown, A. J., Lewis, D., Moberly, R., and Vandekerckhove, W., eds. (2014). *International Handbook on Whistleblowing Research*. Cheltenham: Edward Elgar

Brownlee, K. (2016). The Civil Disobedience of Edward Snowden. *Philosophy and Social Criticism*, 42(10), pp. 965–70

Brenkert, G. G. (2010). Whistle-blowing, Moral Integrity,

and Organizational Ethics. In G. G. Brenkert and T. L. Beauchamp, eds., *Oxford Handbook of Business Ethics*. New York: Oxford University Press, pp. 563–601

Ceva, E. (2016). *Interactive Justice: A Proceduralist Approach to Value Conflict in Politics*. London: Routledge

Ceva, E. (2018). Political Corruption as a Relational Injustice. *Social Philosophy and Policy*, 41(1), pp. 26–50

Ceva, E. and Bocchiola, M. (forthcoming). Personal Trust, Public Accountability, and the Justification of Whistleblowing. *Journal of Political Philosophy*.

Ceva, E. and Ferretti, M. P. (2014). Liberal Democratic Institutions and the Damages of Political Corruption. *Les ateliers de l'éthique / The Ethics Forum*, 9(1), pp. 126–45

Ceva, E. and Ferretti, M. P. (2017). Political Corruption. *Philosophy Compass*, 12(12), pp. 1–10

Ceva, E. and Ferretti, M. P. (2018). Political Corruption, Individual Behaviour and the Quality of Institutions. *Politics, Philosophy & Economics*, 17(2), pp. 216–31

Chambers, A. (1995). Whistleblowing and the Internal Auditor. *Business Ethics: A European Review* 4(4), pp. 192–8

Chandler, R. (1953). *The Long Goodbye*. London: Penguin Books

Davis, M. (1996). Some Paradoxes of Whistleblowing. *Business and Professional Ethics Journal*, 15(1), pp. 3–19

Davis, M. (2003). Whistleblowing. In H. LaFollette, ed., *Oxford Handbook of Practical Ethics*. New York: Oxford University Press, pp. 539–63

DeCew, J. (1997). *In Pursuit of Privacy: Law, Ethics, and the Rise of Technology*. Ithaca: Cornell University Press

De George, R. T. (1981). Ethical Responsibility of Engineers in Large Organizations: The Pinto Case. *Business & Professional Ethics Journal*, 1(1), pp. 1–14

De George, R.T. (2010). Whistle Blowing. In *Business Ethics*, 7th edn. New York: Macmillan, pp. 298–318

References

Delmas, C. (2015). The Ethics of Government Whistleblowing. *Social Theory and Practice*, 41(1), pp. 77–105

Fabre, C. (2002). Good Samaritanism: A Matter of Justice. *Critical Review of International Social and Political Philosophy*, 25(2), pp. 241–64

Feinberg, J. (1990). *The Moral Limits of Criminal Law*, vol. IV: *Harmless Wrongdoing*. Oxford University Press

Flathman, R. E. (1966). *The Public Interest: An Essay Concerning the Normative Discourse of Politics*. New York: Wiley

Gall, C. and Shah, T. (2009). Afghans Recall Airstrike Horror, and Fault US. *The New York Times* (online), p. A1, www.nytimes.com/2009/05/15/world/asia/15farah.html

Glazer, M. P. and Glazer, P. M. (1989). *The Whistle-Blowers: Exposing Corruption in Government and Industry*. New York: Basic Books

Greenwald, G. (2013). NSA Collecting Phone Records of Millions of Verizon Customers Daily. *The Guardian* (online), https://www.theguardian.com/world/2013/jun/06/nsa-phone-records-verizon-court-order

Hart, H. L. A. (2008). *Punishment and Responsibility: Essays in the Philosophy of Law*. Oxford University Press

Held, V. (1970). *The Public Interest and Individual Interests*. New York: Basic Books

Hoffman, W. Michael and Schwartz, Mark S. (2015). The Morality of Whistleblowing: A Commentary on Richard. T. De George. *Journal of Business Ethics*, 127(4), pp. 771–781

Hood, C. and Heald, D., eds. (2006). *Transparency: The Key to Better Governance*. Oxford University Press.

Inness, J. C. (1992). *Privacy, Intimacy and Isolation*. Oxford University Press

Jubb, P. (1999). Whistleblowing: A Restrictive Definition and Interpretation. *Journal of Business Ethics*, 21(1), pp. 77–94

King, S. M., Bradley, S. C. and Roberts, G. E. (2010). Reflections

References

on Defining the Public Interest. *Administration & Society*, 41(8), pp. 954–78

Kumar, M. and Santoro, D. (2017). A Justification of Whistleblowing. *Philosophy & Social Criticism*, 43(7), pp. 669–84

Leigh, D., Ball, J., Cobain, I. and Burke, J. (2011). Guantánamo Leaks Lift Lid on World's Most Controversial Prison. *The Guardian* (online), https://www.theguardian.com/world/2011/apr/25/guantanamo-files-lift-lid-prison

Lepora, C. and Goodin, R. E. (2013). *On Complicity and Compromise*. Oxford University Press

Lewis, D., Brown, A. J., and Moberly, R. (2014). Whisteblowing, its Importance and the State of the Research. In A. J. Brown, D. Lewis, R. Moberly, and W. Vandekerckhove, eds., *International Handbook on Whistleblowing Research*. Cheltenham: Edward Elgar, pp. 1–34

Leys, J. and Vandekerckhove, W. (2014). Whistleblowing Duties. In A. J. Brown, D. Lewis, R. Moberly, and W. Vandekerckhove, eds., *International Handbook on Whistleblowing Research*. Cheltenham: Edward Elgar, pp. 115–32

Meyers, S. L. (2010). US Soldier Is Charged with Viewing Secret Cables. *The New York Times*, (online), p. A4, www.nytimes.com/2010/07/07/world/middleeast/07wikileaks.html

Miceli, M. P. and Near, J. P. (1992). *Blowing the Whistle: The Organizational and Legal Implications for Companies and Employees*. New York: Lexington Books

Miceli, M. P., Dreyfus, S. and Near, J. P. (2014). Outsider 'Whistleblowers': Conceptualizing and Distinguishing 'Bell-Ringing' Behavior. In A. J. Brown, D. Lewis, R. Moberly, and W. Vandekerckhove, eds. *International Handbook on Whistleblowing Research*. Cheltenham: Edward Elgar, pp. 71–94

Miller, S. (2014). Social Institutions. In N. Zalta, ed., *The*

References

Stanford Encyclopedia of Philosophy (online), https://plato.stanford.edu/archives/win2014/entries/social-institutions

Miller, S. (2017). *Institutional Corruption.* Cambridge University Press

Mokrosińska, D. (2017). Privacy and Autonomy: On Some Misconceptions Concerning the Political Dimensions of Privacy. *Law and Philosophy*, https://doi.org/10.1007/s10982-017-9307-3

Moore, A. D. (2010). *Privacy Rights: Moral and Legal Foundations.* University Park: Penn State University Press

Near, J. P. and Miceli, M. P. (1985). Organizational Dissidence: The Case of Whistle-Blowing. *Journal of Business Ethics*, 4(1), pp. 1–16

O'Neill, O. (2006). Transparency and the Ethics of Communication. In C. Hood and D. Heald, eds., *Transparency: The Key to Better Governance.* Oxford University Press, pp. 75–90.

Rachels, J. (1975). Why Privacy is Important. *Philosophy and Public Affairs*, 4(4), pp. 323–33

Raz, J. (1979). *The Authority of Law.* Oxford University Press

Raz, J. (1986). *The Morality of Freedom.* Oxford University Press

Sagar, R. (2013). *Secrets and Leak:. The Dilemma of State Secrecy.* Princeton University Press

Scheuerman, W. E. (2014). Whistleblowing as Civil Disobedience: The Case of Edward Snowden. *Philosophy and Social Criticism*, 40(7), pp. 609–28.

Seglow, J. (2004). *The Ethics of Altruism.* London: Taylor & Francis

Singer, P. (1972). Famine, Affluence, and Morality. *Philosophy & Public Affairs* 1(3), pp. 229–43

Singer, P. (2009). *The Life You Can Save: Acting Now to End World Poverty.* New York: Random House

References

Solove, D. (2008). *Understanding Privacy*. Cambridge, MA: Harvard University Press

Solove, D. (2011). *Nothing to Hide: The False Trade-off Between Privacy and Security*. New Haven: Yale University Press

Thompson, D. T. (1999). Democratic Secrecy. *Political Science Quarterly*, 114(2), pp. 181–93

Tsahuridu, E. E. and Vandekerckhove, W. (2008). Organizational Whistleblowing Policies: Making Employees Responsible or Liable? *Journal of Business Ethics*, 82(1), pp. 107–18

Vandekerckhove, W. (2006). *Whistleblowing and Organizational Social Responsibility*. Aldershot: Ashgate

Vandekerckhove, W. and Tsahuridu, E. E. (2010). Risky Rescues and the Duty to Blow the Whistle. *Journal of Business Ethics*, 97(3), pp. 365–80

Westin, A. F. (1981). *Whistle-Blowing! Loyalty and Dissent in the Corporation*. New York: McGraw-Hill, 1981

WikiLeaks (2010a). *Kabul War Diary* (online), https://wikileaks.org/afg

WikiLeaks (2010b). *Baghdad War Diary* (online), https://wikileaks.org/irq

WikiLeaks (2010c). *Cablegate,* https://wikileaks.org/plusd/?q project[]=cg&q=#result

WikiLeaks (2011). *About* (online), https://wikileaks.org/About.html

Wodehouse, P. G. (2010). *Right Ho, Jeeves*. Auckland: The Floating Press